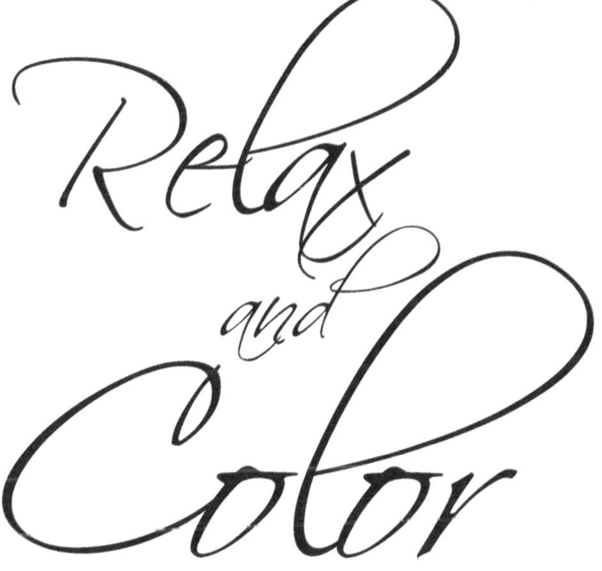

Relax and Color

An Oasis of Me-Time in Your Busy Day

Cara Stein

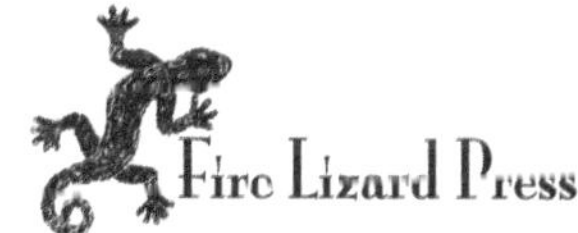

Fire Lizard Press

Relax and Color

First Paperback Edition

Acknowledgements

Big thanks to my family and friends, my book-publishing clients, and everyone at 17000 Days for your love and support. I couldn't have made this book without you!

Also, special thanks to Johanna Basford for getting everyone excited about coloring again! Secret Garden and Enchanted Forest were a big source of inspiration for this book.

Finally, thank you, dear reader! I've poured my heart into this book. I hope you love it as much as I do.

Introduction

Welcome to Relax and Color! In the words of Ferriss Bueller,

> Life moves pretty fast. If you don't stop and
> look around once in a while, you could miss it.

We all have too many responsibilities, too many interruptions, and too much to do. In the midst of taking care of everyone and everything else, it's easy to lose sight of ourselves.

I created this book for you, and also for me. I needed a way to take a tiny vacation in the middle of my regular life. I needed a way to unwind and clear my head without needing any special equipment or knowledge. And I wanted a simple way to exercise my creativity.

Children love coloring for all of these reasons. As adults, we often lose sight of the simple pleasures, but coloring is one that's always waiting for us. I'm delighted to share this book with you, and I hope you enjoy it as much as I do.

You don't need any special talent, skills, or equipment to color these pages. Anyone can color! Just get some markers or colored pencils and get started. (If you're using markers, you may want to put a blank piece of paper behind the page you're coloring, in case the ink bleeds through.)

Most importantly, remember: this is a chance to do exactly what you want. Be as delicate or as wild as you want. Let this be one area in your life where you forget all about constraints, judgment, or perfection. Just enjoy yourself.

I've set up the pages so that the designs are only on one side of the page. That way, you can color all you like without having to worry about the ink bleeding through to other designs. I've also included quotes and ideas that I've found inspiring, so you can think about something positive while you color.

Remember, this is your book. If you would rather have loose pages than a bound book, then take the book apart. You can do this by breaking the spine and then using scissors or a sharp knife and straightedge to remove the pages. If you want to copy individual pages for your own use, you're welcome to do that, but please don't copy them for other uses without permission. (If you need permission, please write to info@17000-days.com with your request.)

If you like this book and want to check out more of my work, you can find me on http://17000-days.com

Thanks! Happy coloring!
Cara

What small change would make a big, positive
impact on your life right now?

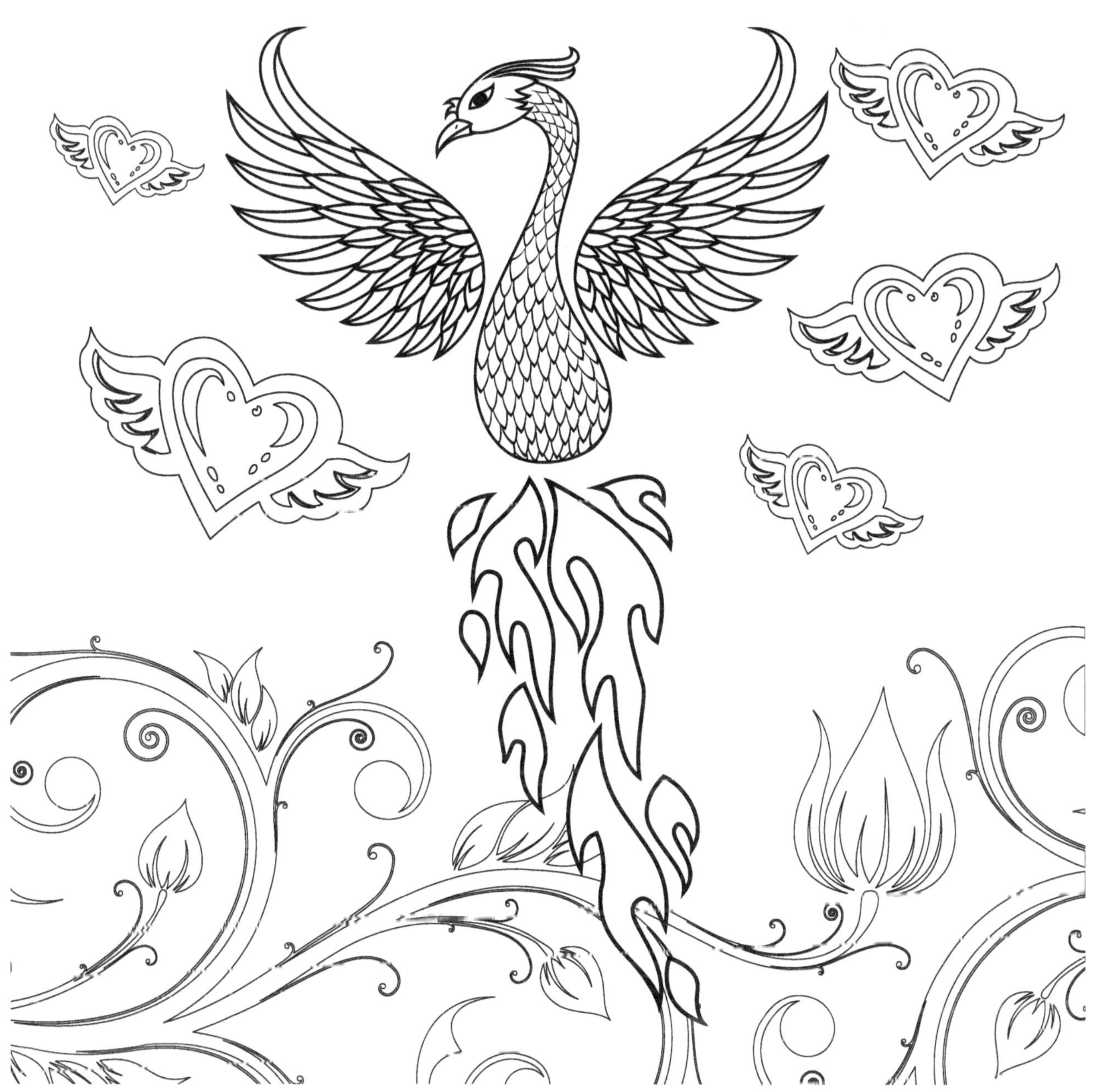

You cannot always know how things are meant to unfold in your best interest, but they always do, even when things seem bleak. What you can know, however, is that it is perfectly safe and helpful to relax all attachment to outcome, and instead invest that energy in choosing your preferred state of being.

Don't mind the circumstances, they are not in your control. Mind only your state of being, for that is your only job.

– Free Awareness Foundation

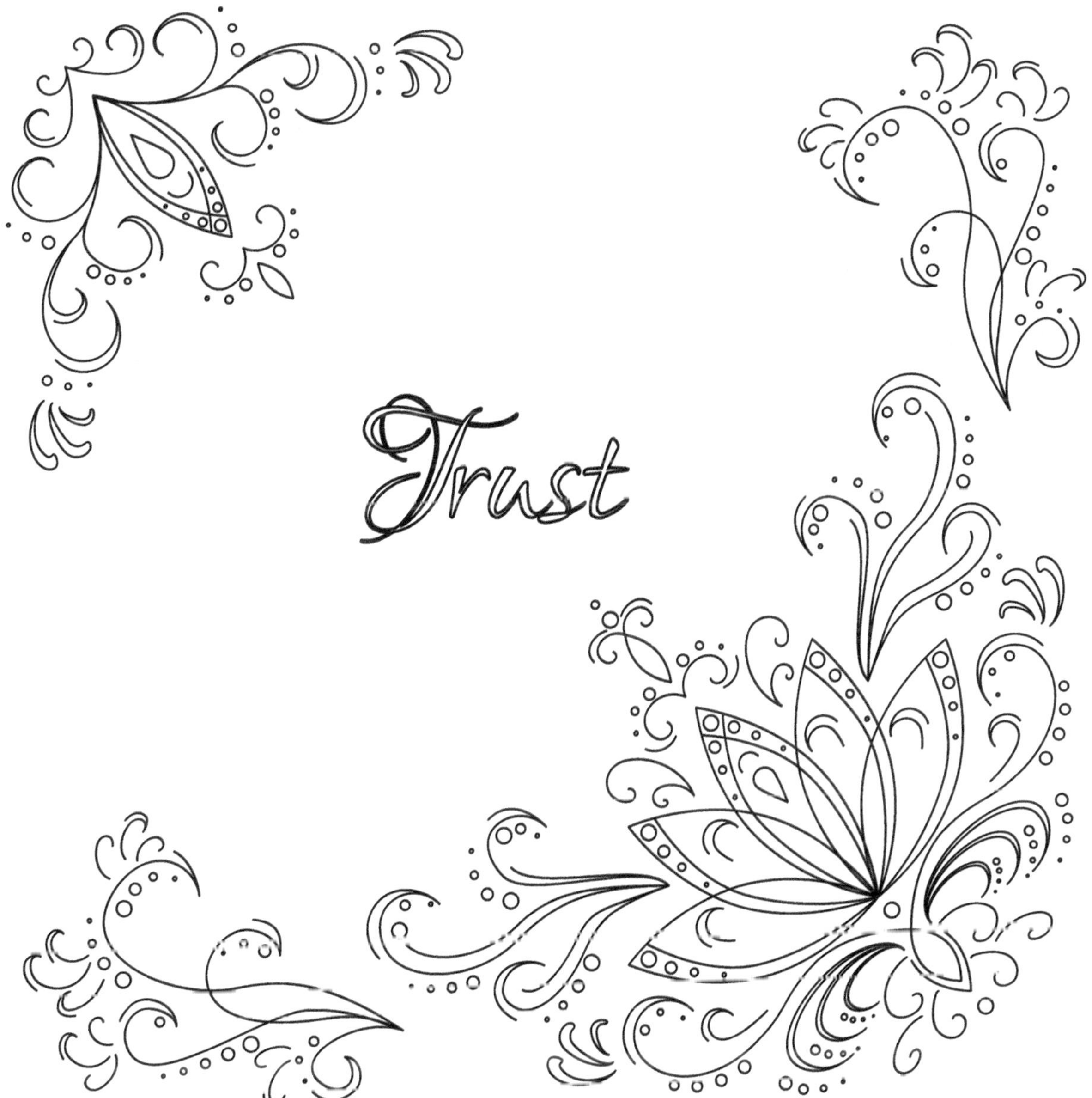

Trust

Listen to your own voice, your own soul. Too many people listen to the noise of the world instead of themselves.

-Prolific Living

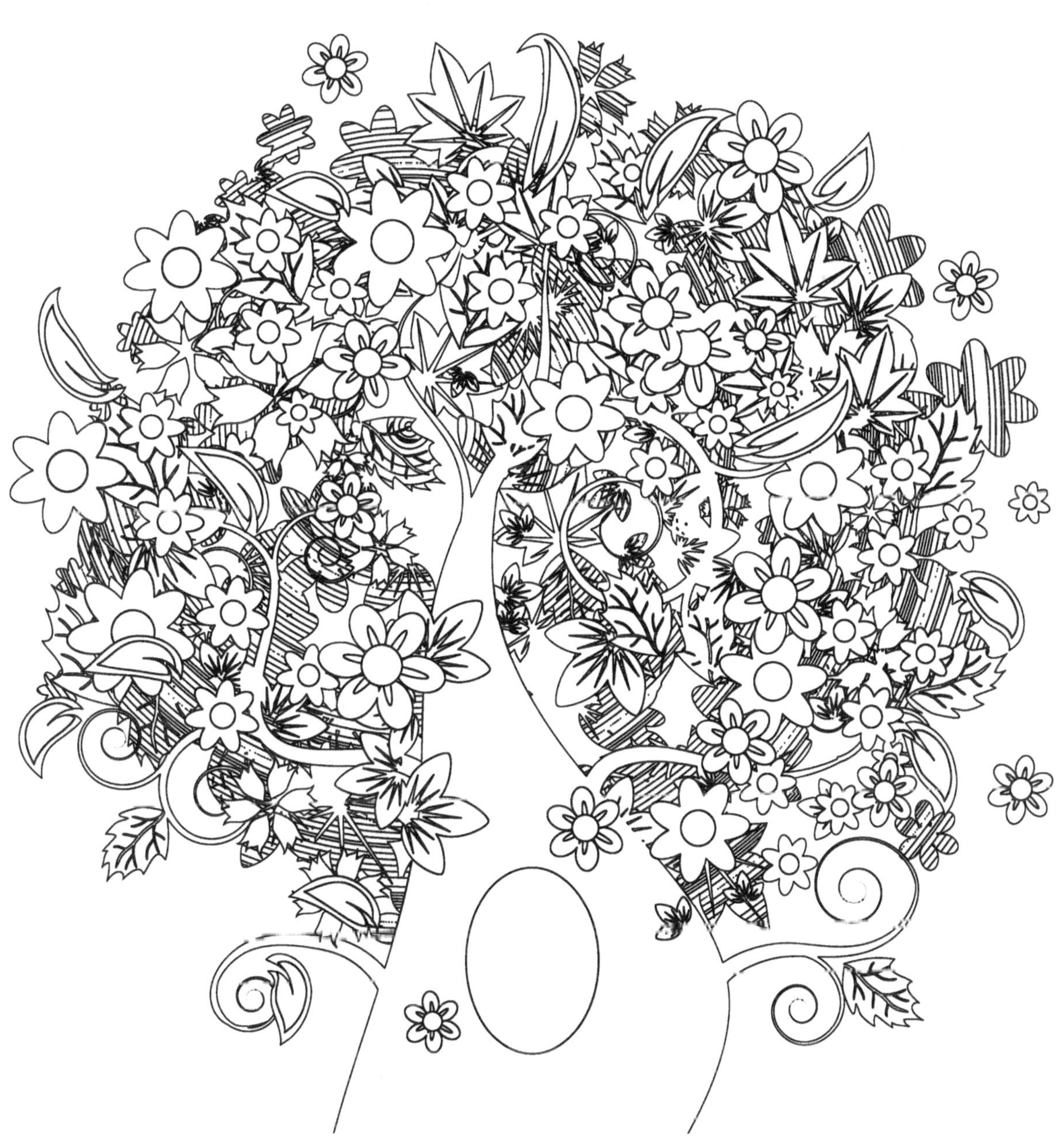

Remain calm in every situation because
peace equals power.

– Joyce Meyer

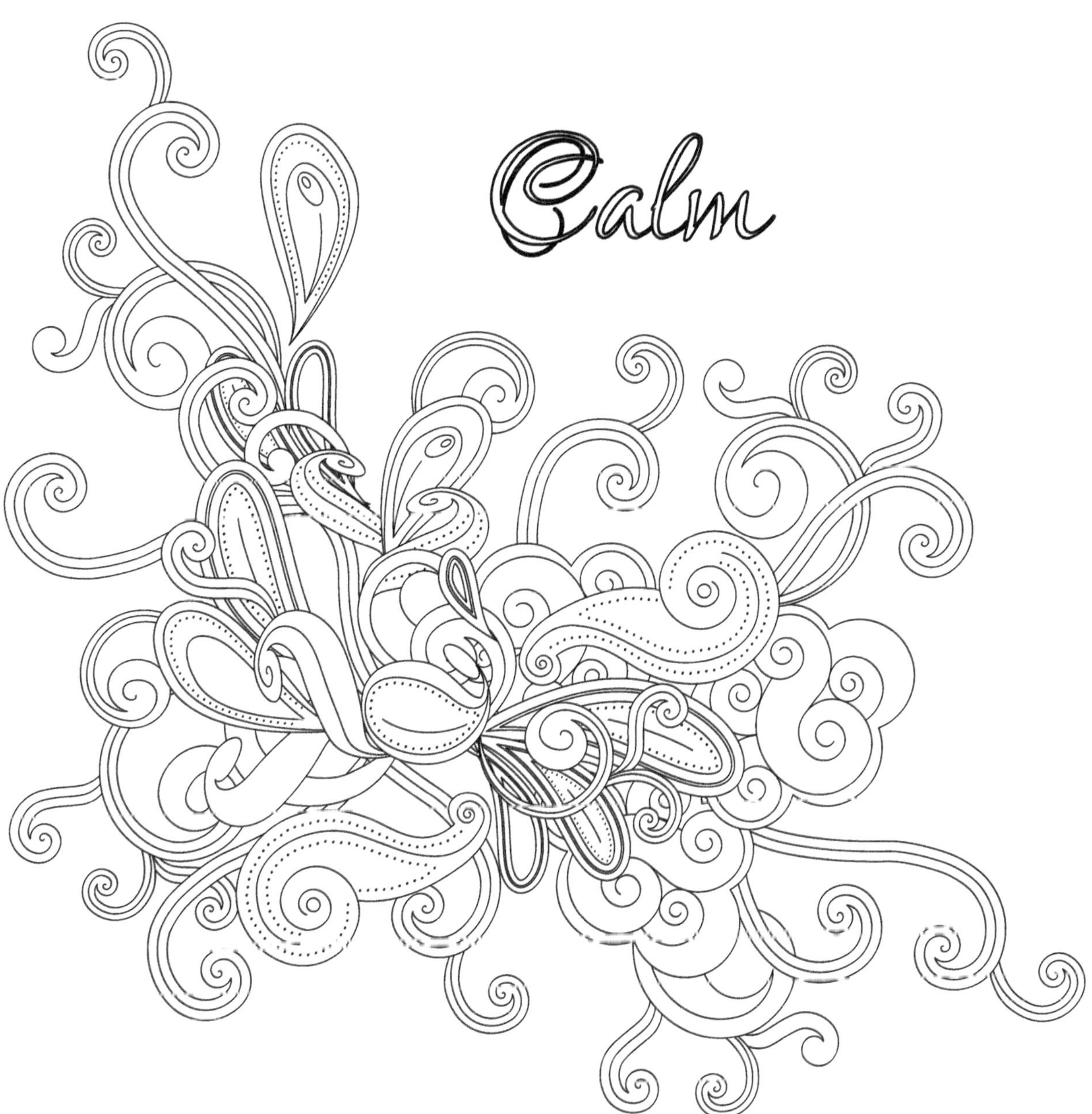

Calm

The greatest healing therapy is friendship and love.

– Hubert H. Humphrey

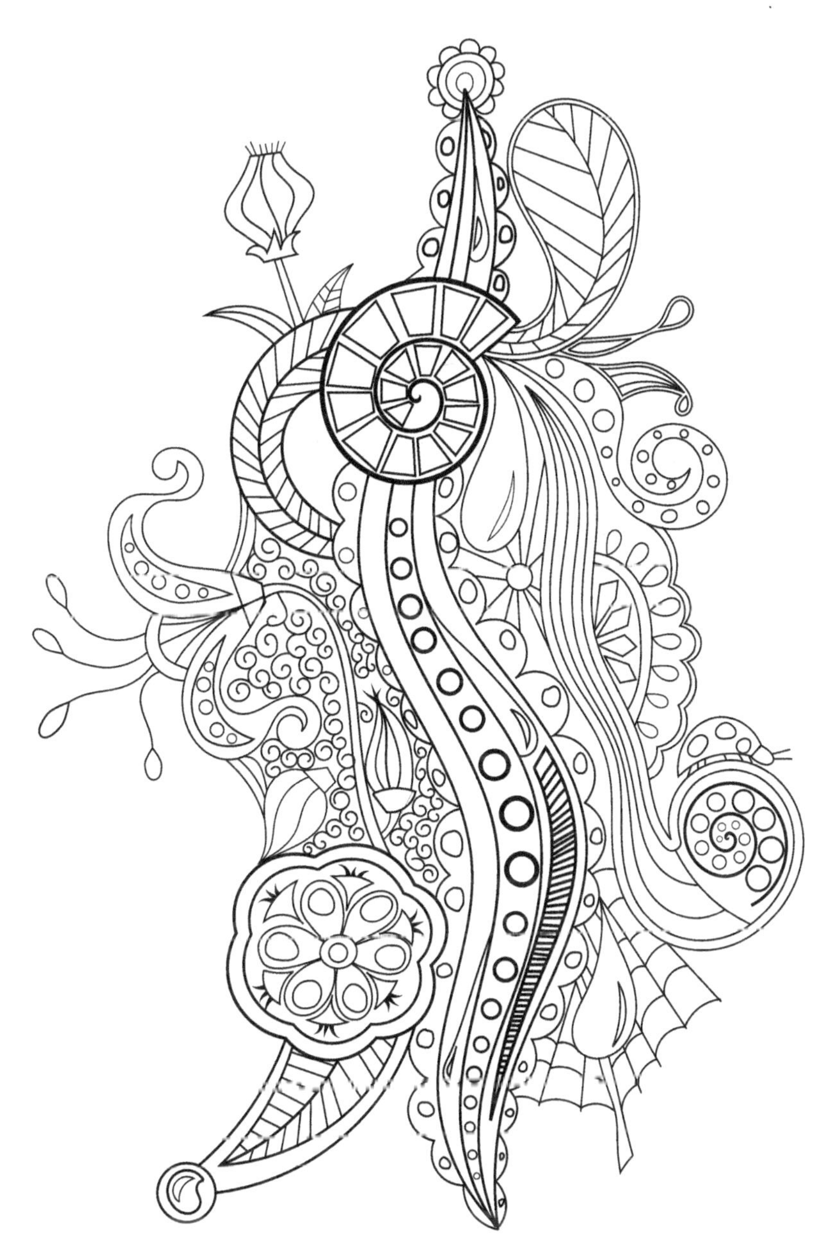

Make a list of all of your responsibilities.
Now cross out everything that feels yucky.
What would it take for you to actually
stop doing these things?

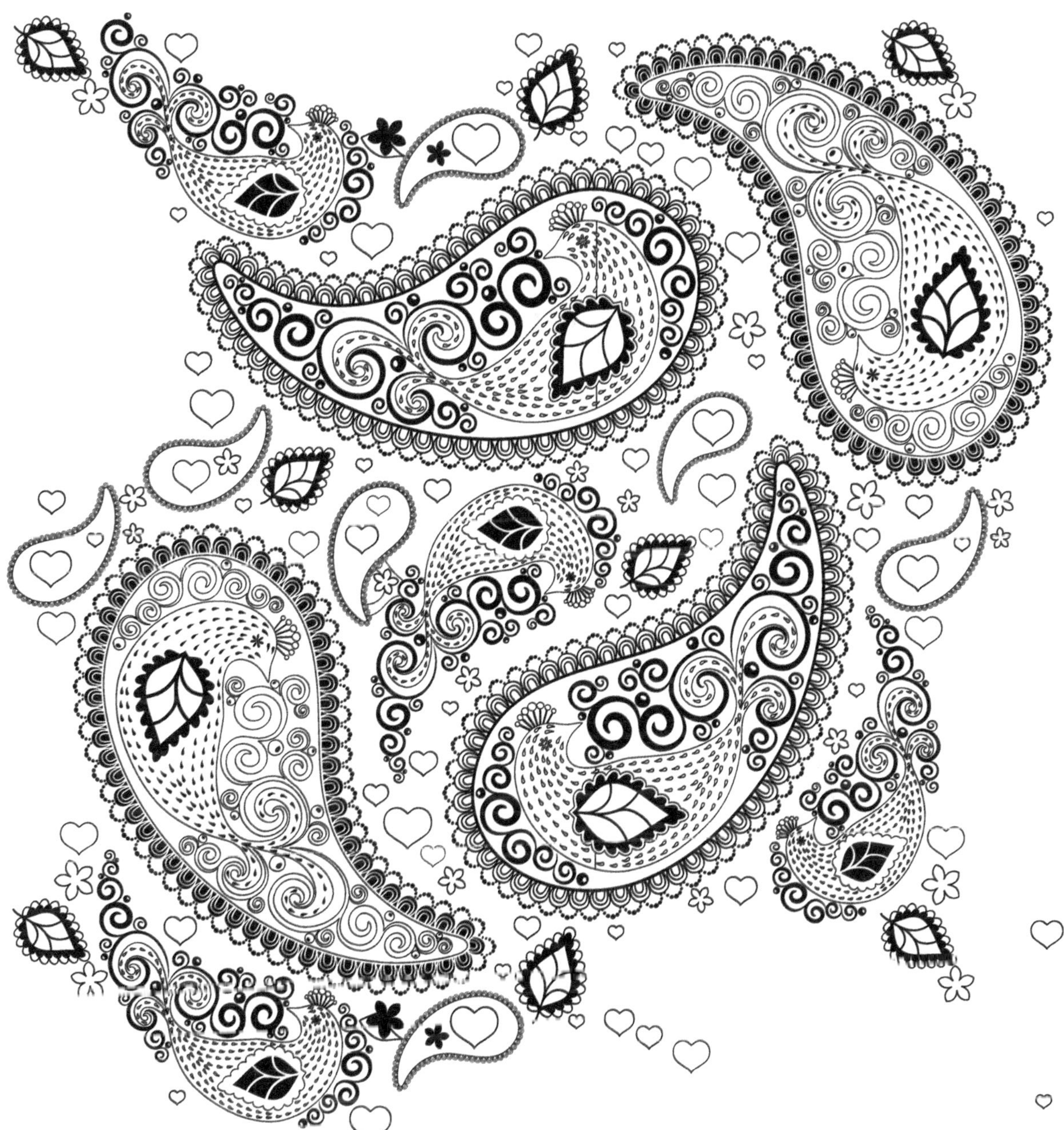

Who can you count on in bad times?

Support

What feels good in your life right now?
What feels bad?

How are you feeling right now?

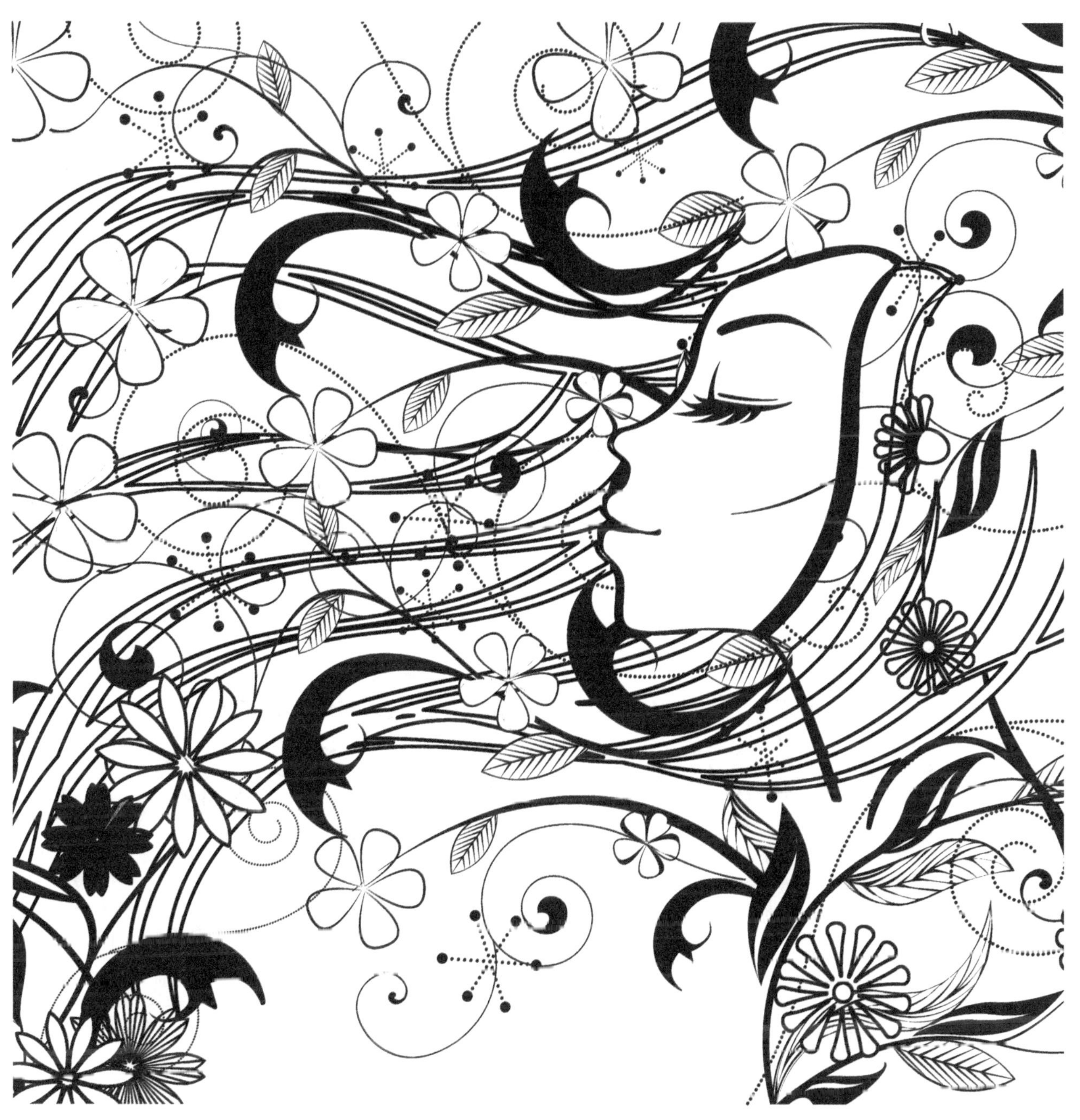

Hanging onto resentment is letting someone you despise
live rent-free in your head.
- Esther Lederer

What grievances are you holding onto?
What would it take for you to let them go?

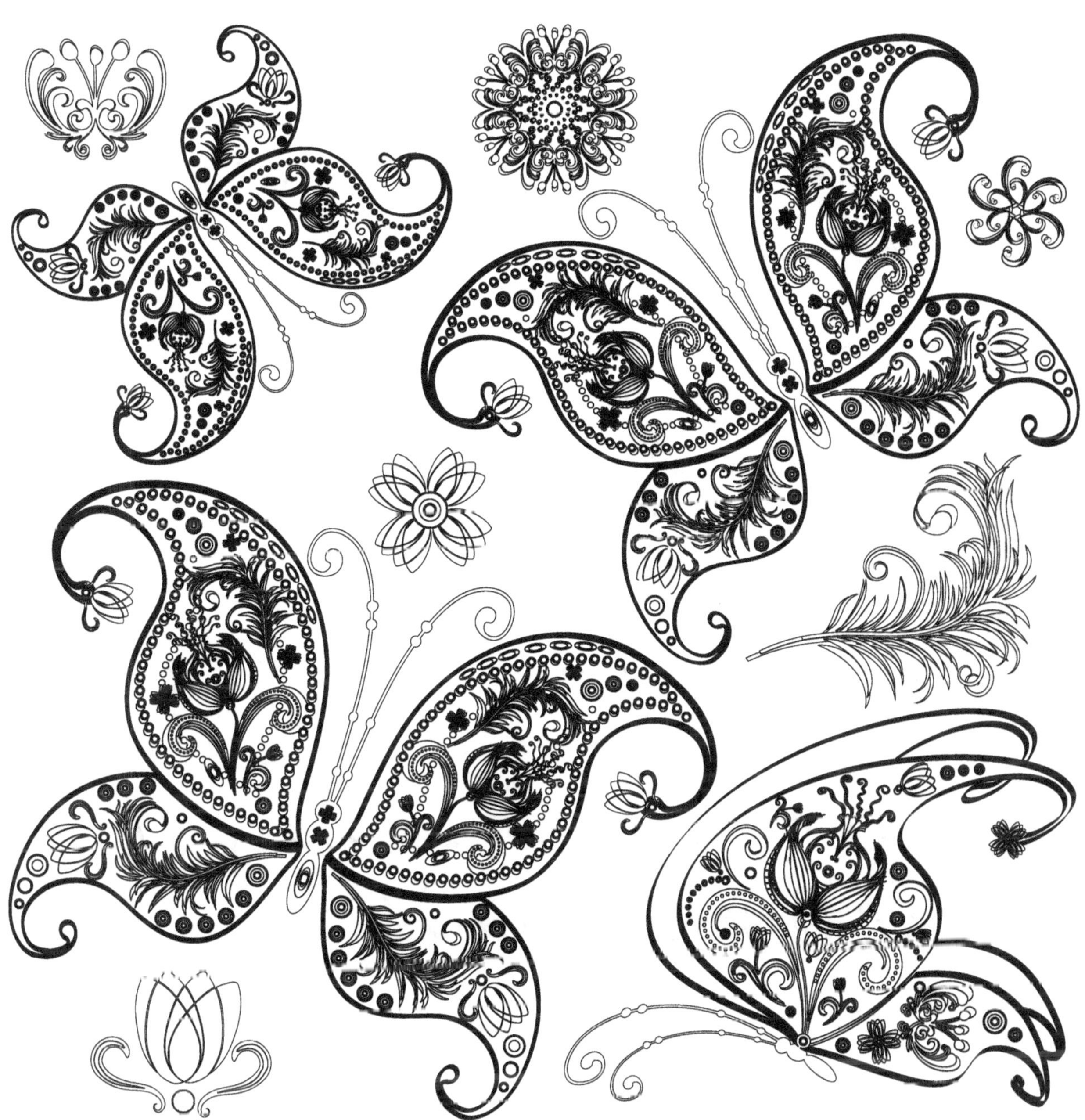

Do you believe we get everything we need?
How does your perspective affect your life?

Think of 10 times when you thought you had
too little of something, but you survived.

Think of 10 things you have too much of now.

Think of 10 wonderful things that entered your life at
just the right time without effort from you.

– Martha Beck

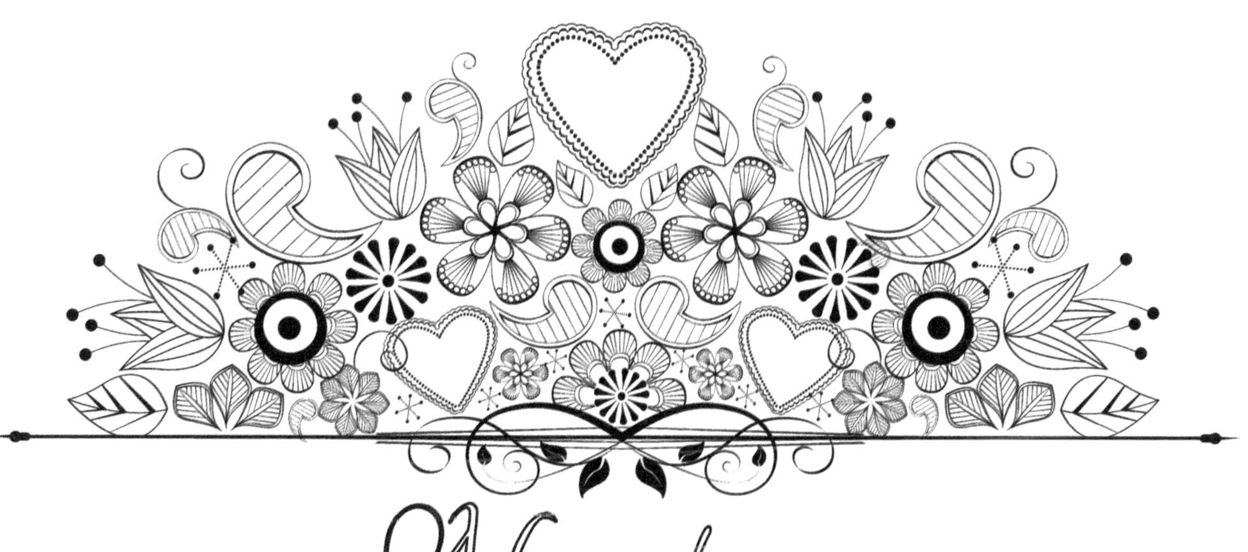

Abundance

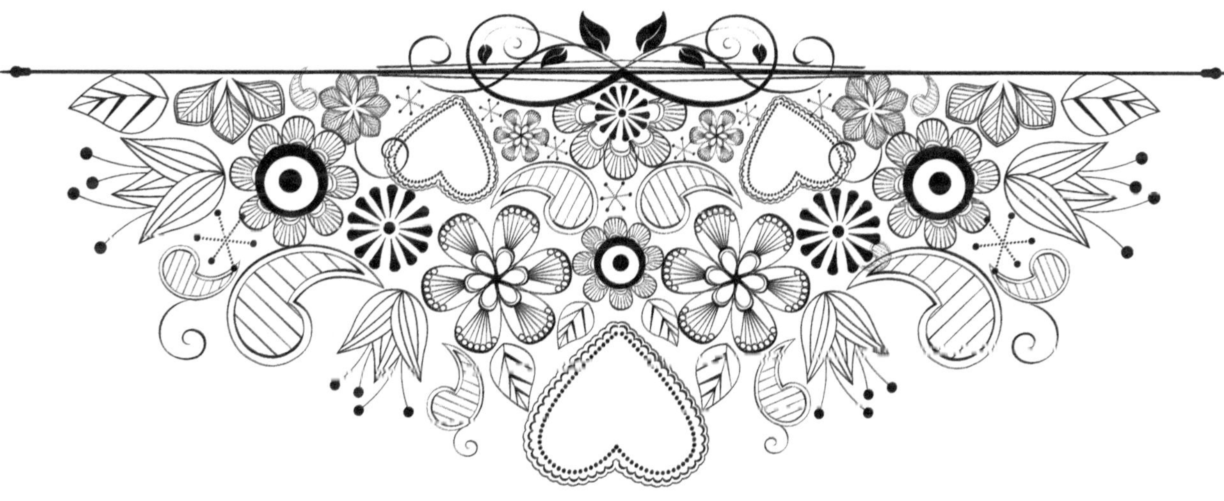

To feel happy and balanced,
what do you want more of in your life?
What do you want less of?

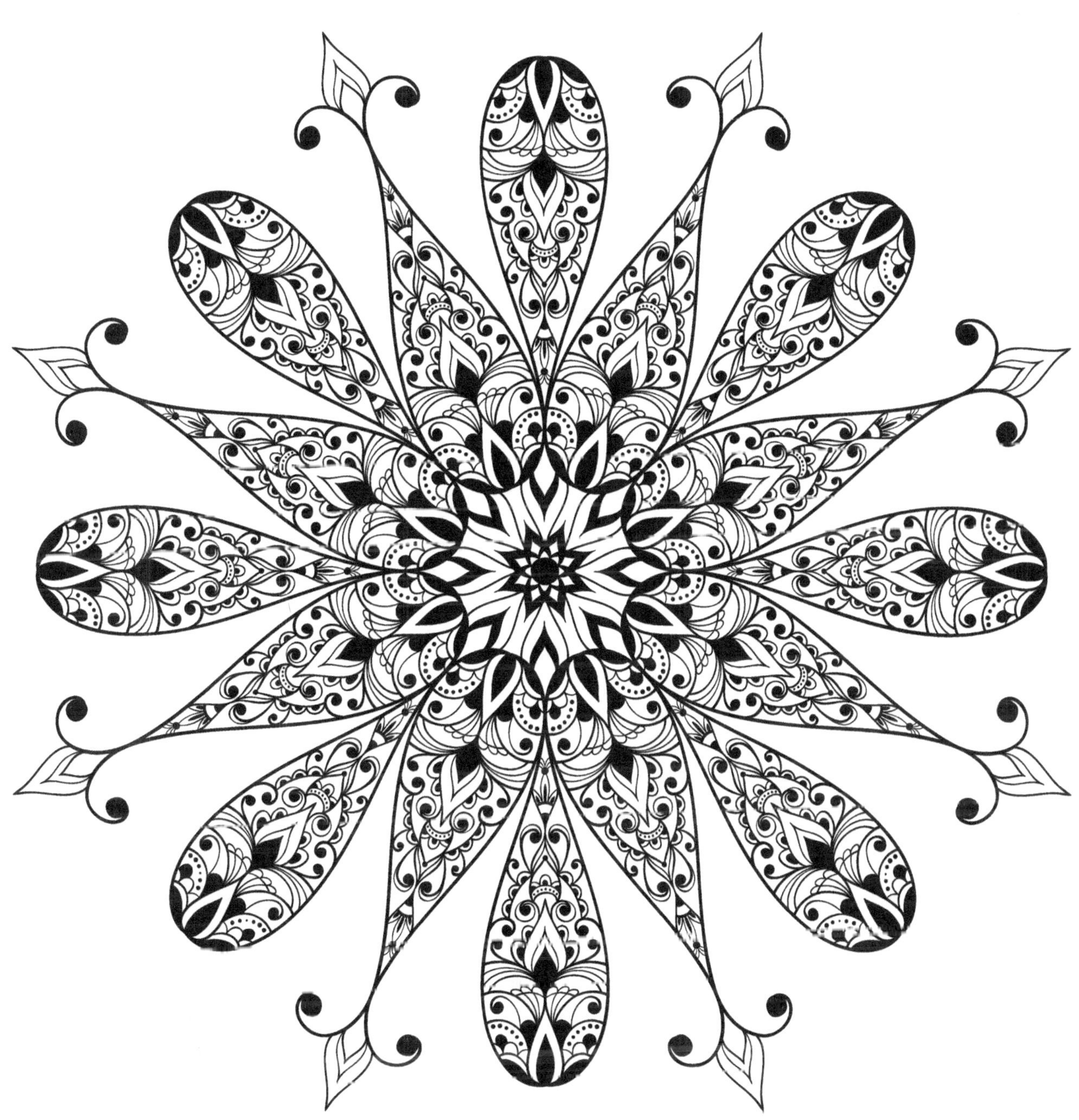

*If money were no object, what would
you do with your time?*

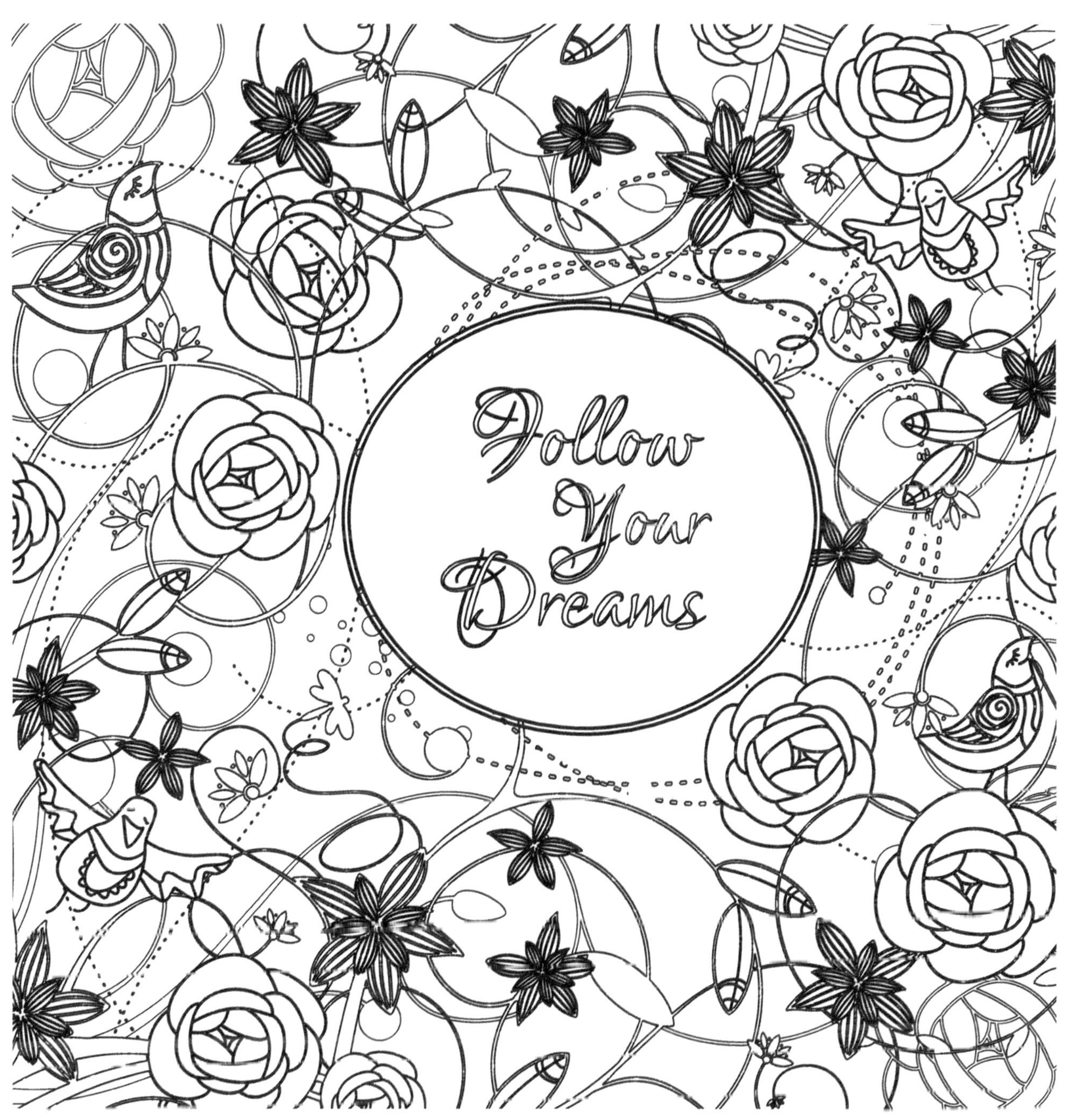
Follow
Your
Dreams

There is a calmness to
a life lived in gratitude,
a quiet joy.

—Ralph H. Blum

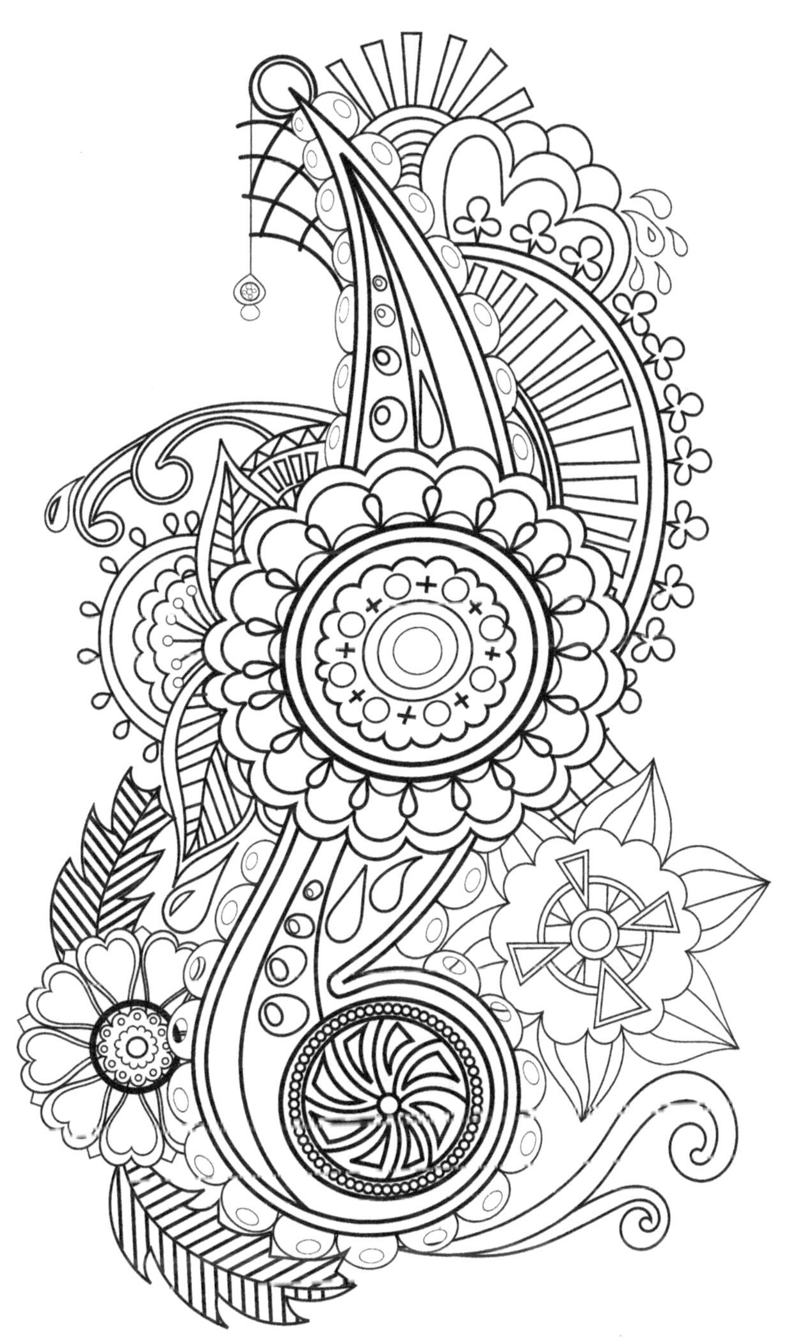

Be content with what you have;
rejoice in the way things are.
When you realize there is nothing lacking,
the whole world belongs to you.

— Lao Tzu

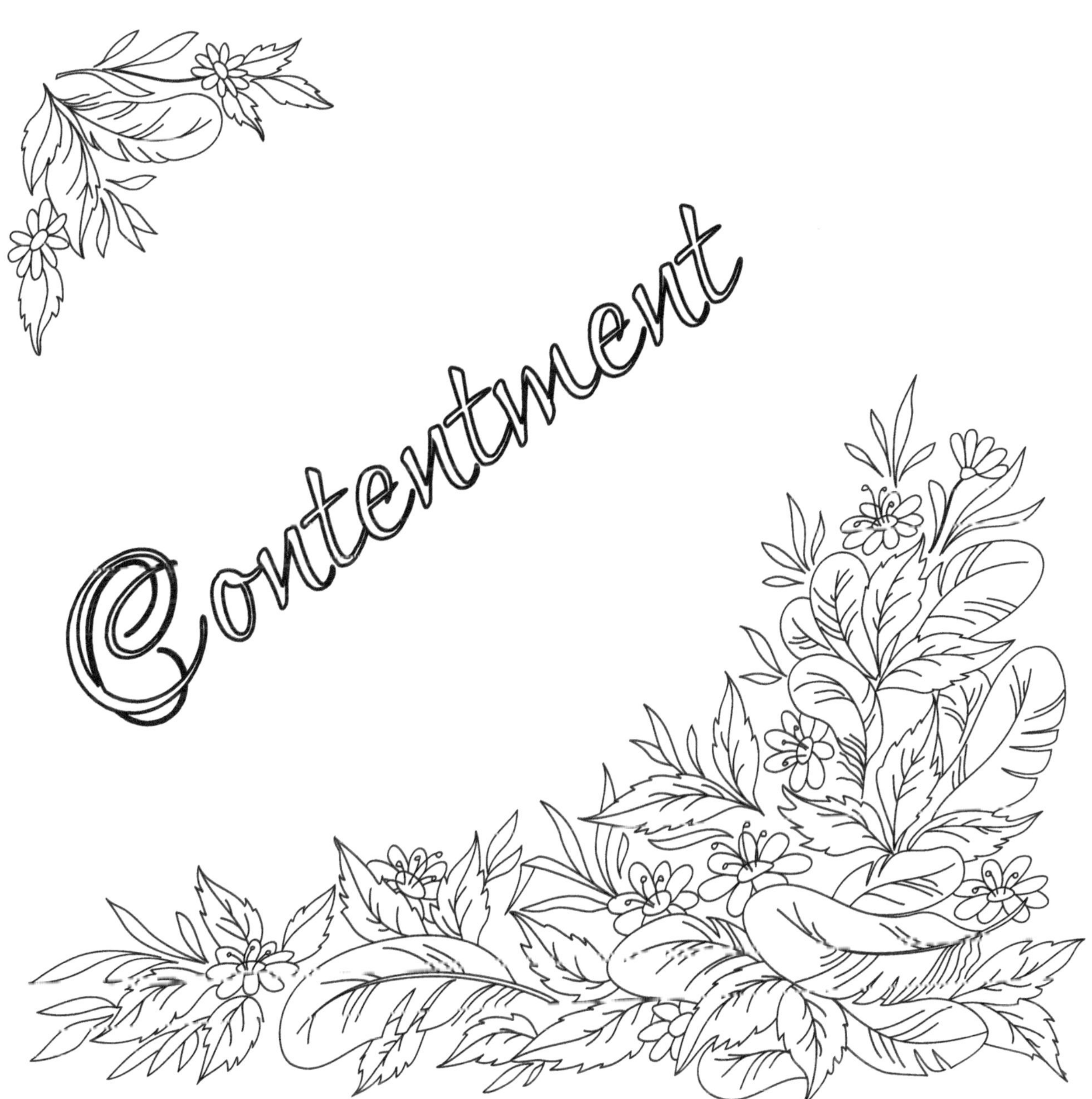

Contentment

Who do you love?
Who loves you?

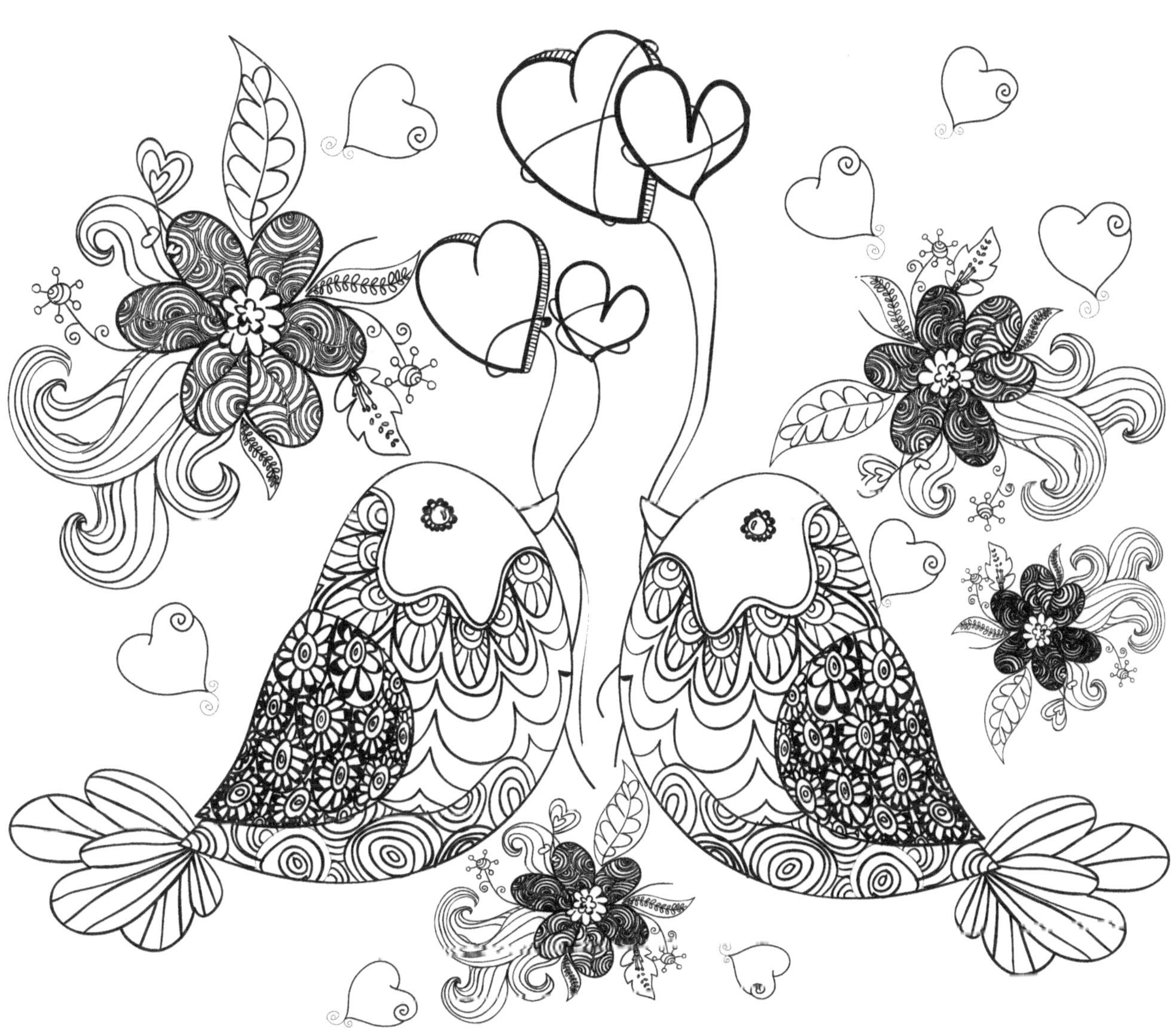

It's difficult to believe in yourself
because the idea of self is an artificial construction.
You are, in fact, part of the
glorious oneness of the universe.
Everything beautiful in the world
is within you.

— Russell Brand

If you could get everyone in the world to agree with you on one thing, what would you want it to be?

– Darla LeDoux

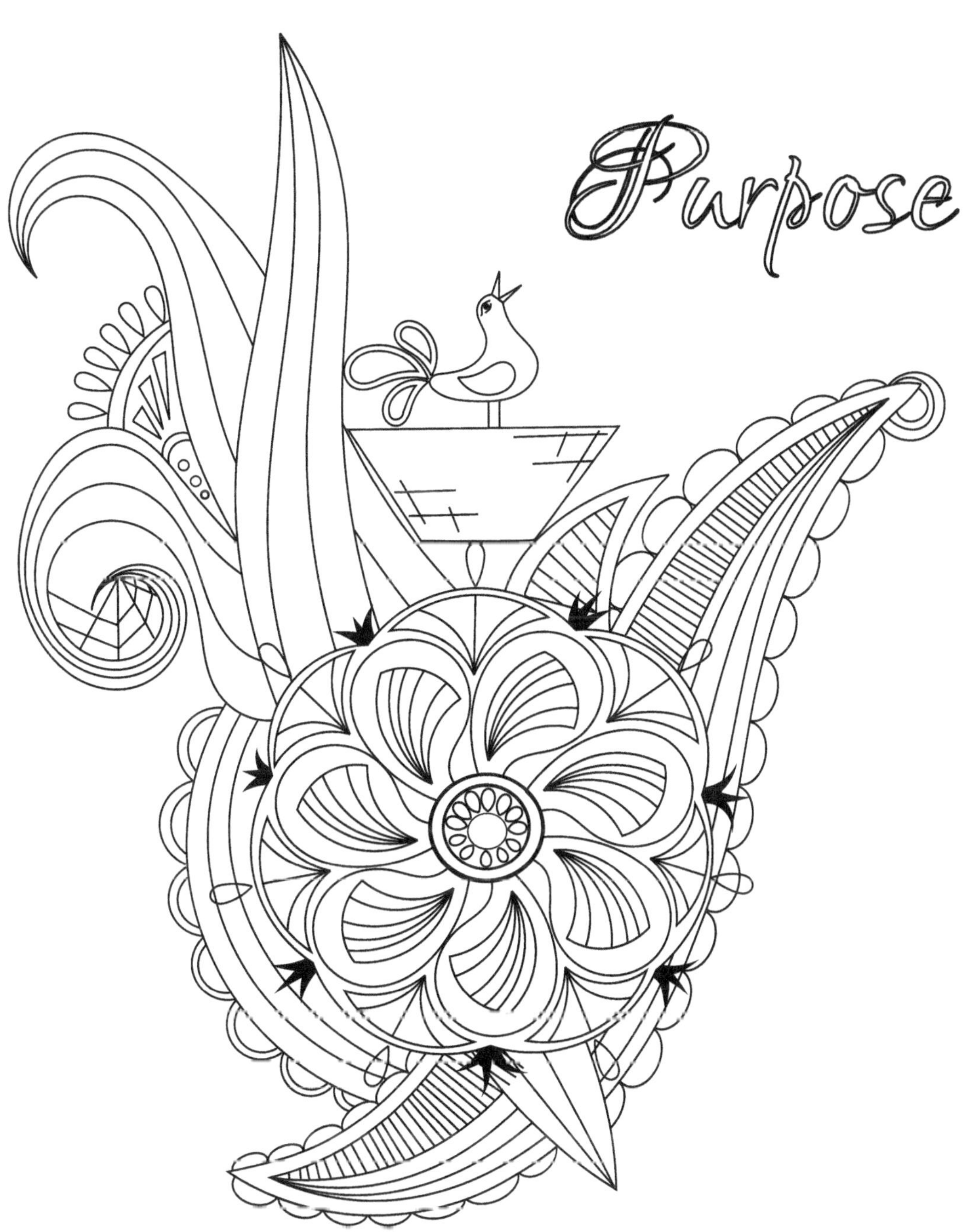

Purpose

What are you uniquely good at?

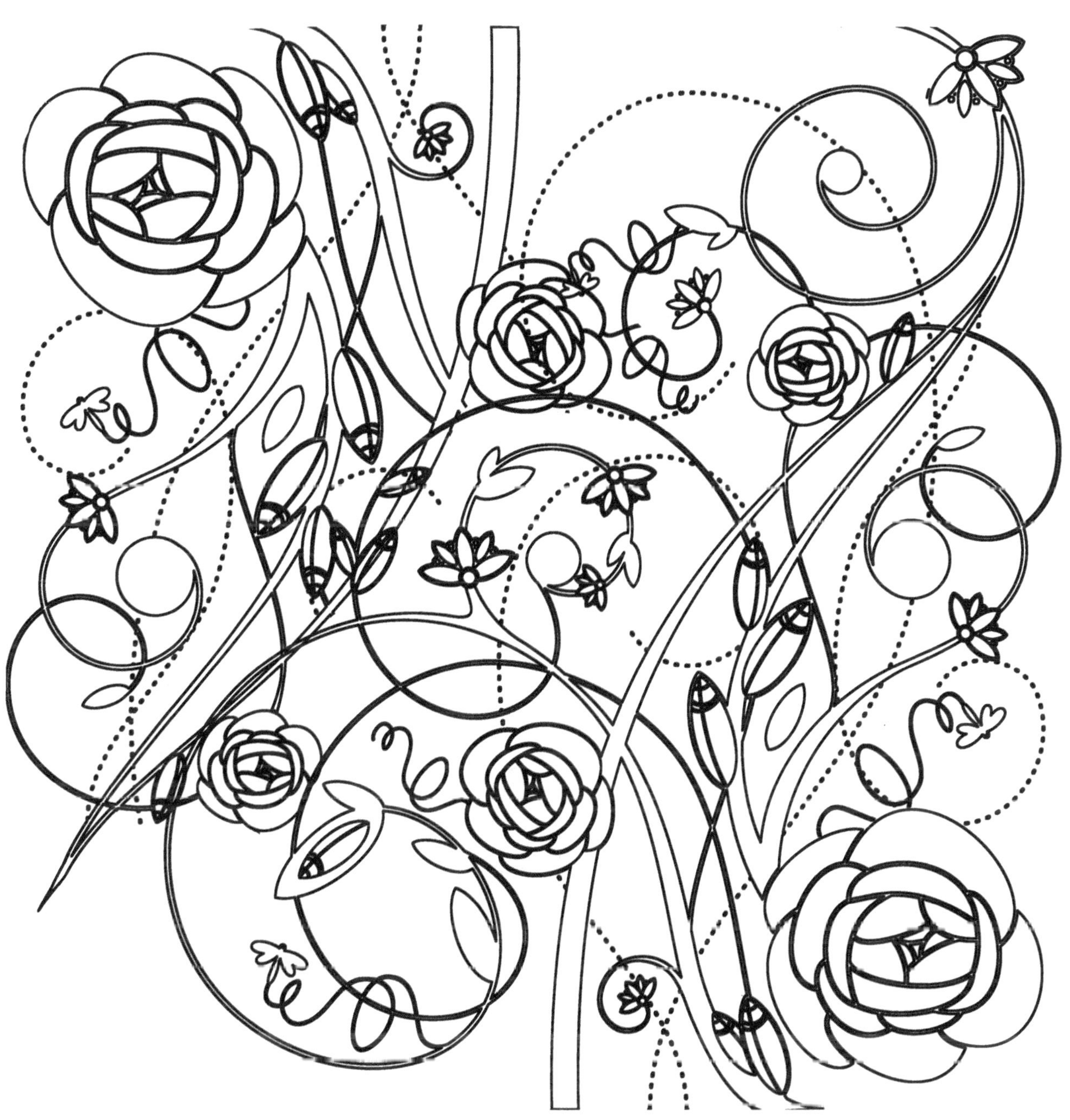

What's most important about you as a person?

Do you love yourself as much as you love the other people in your life?

What do you wish others would say to comfort and support you? How can you give the same thing to yourself?

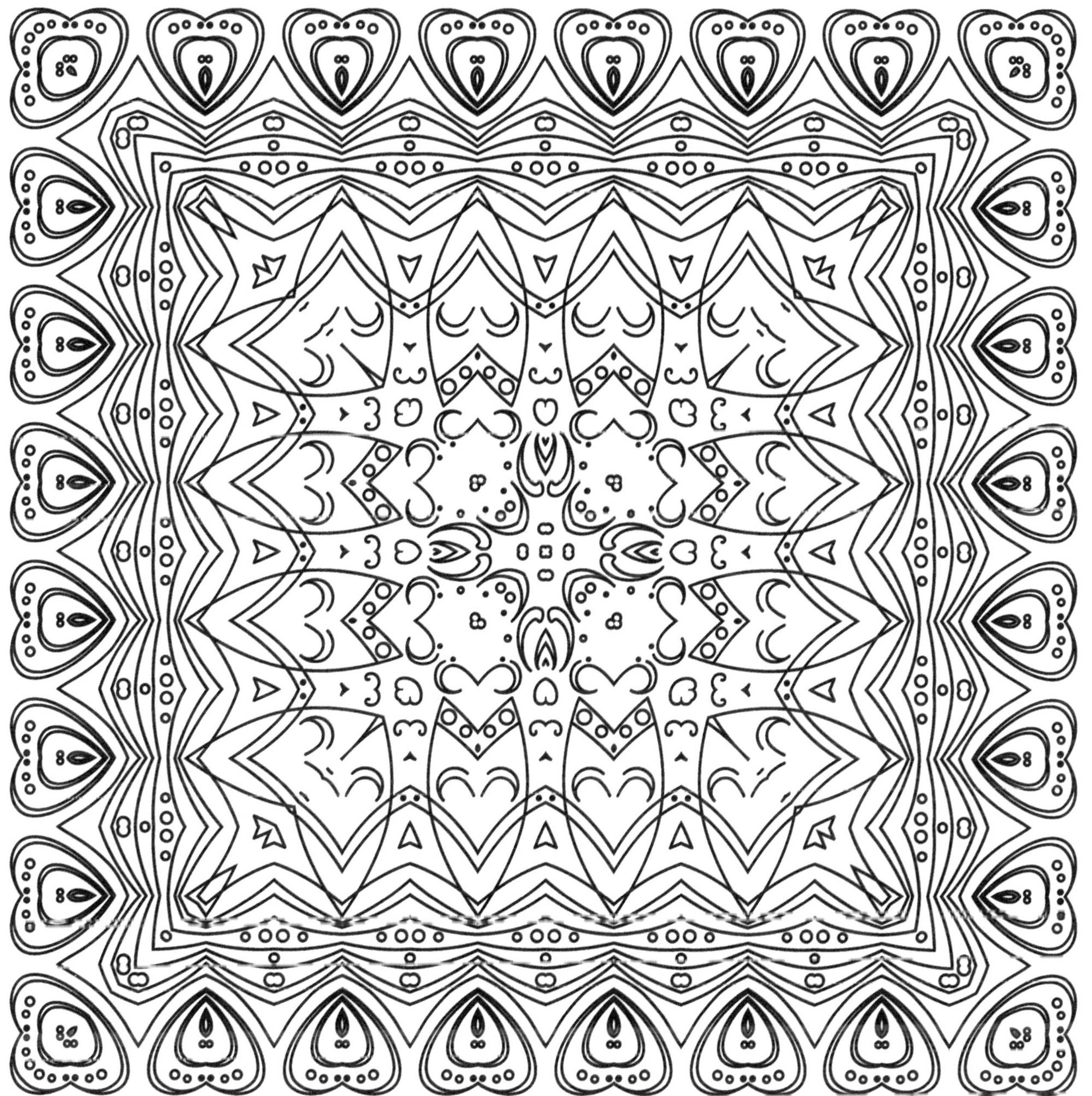

What have you done that you're most proud of?
(today, this week, this month, this year, this life)

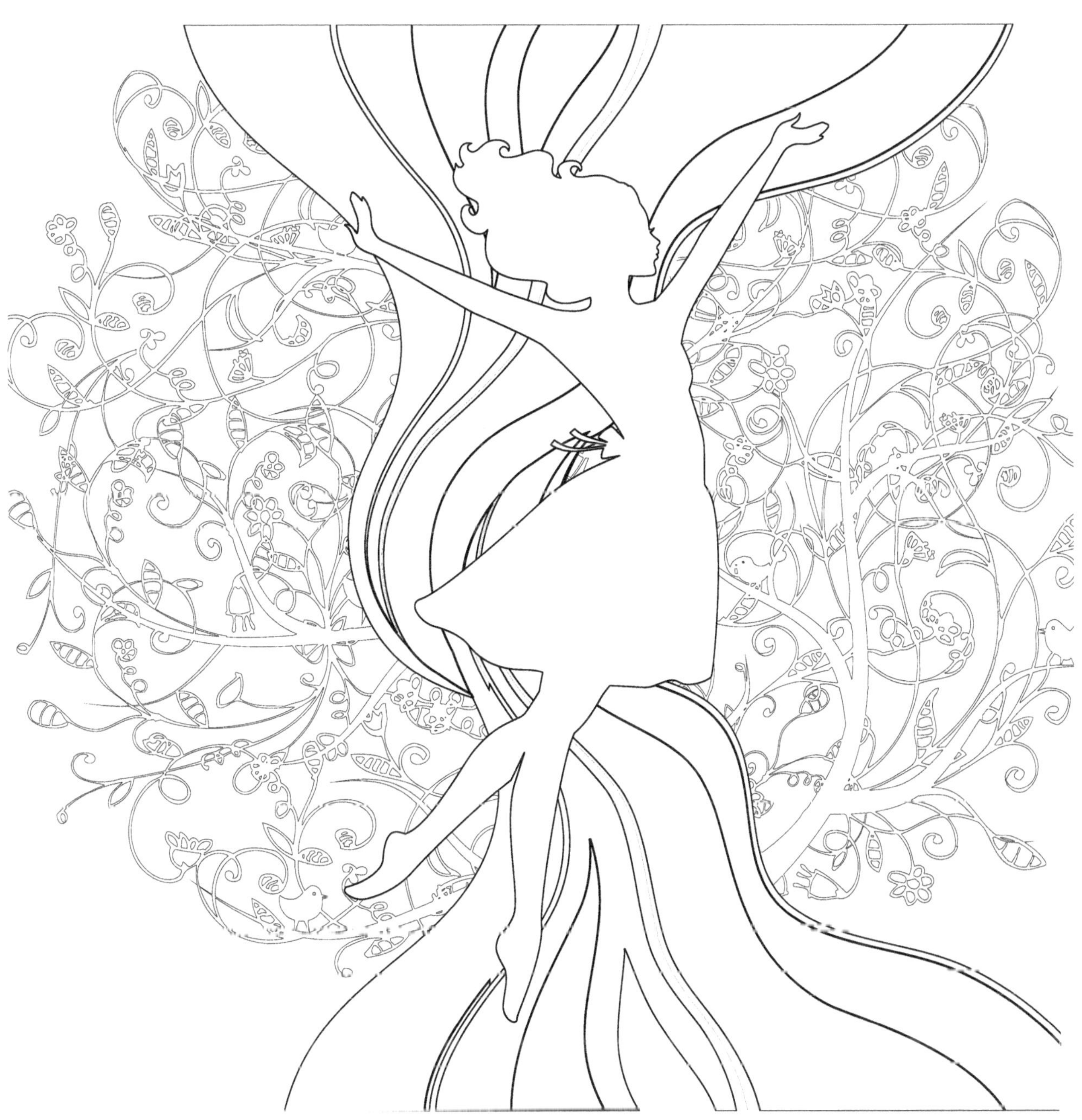

If you could change anything about yourself, what would you change? How would that help you?

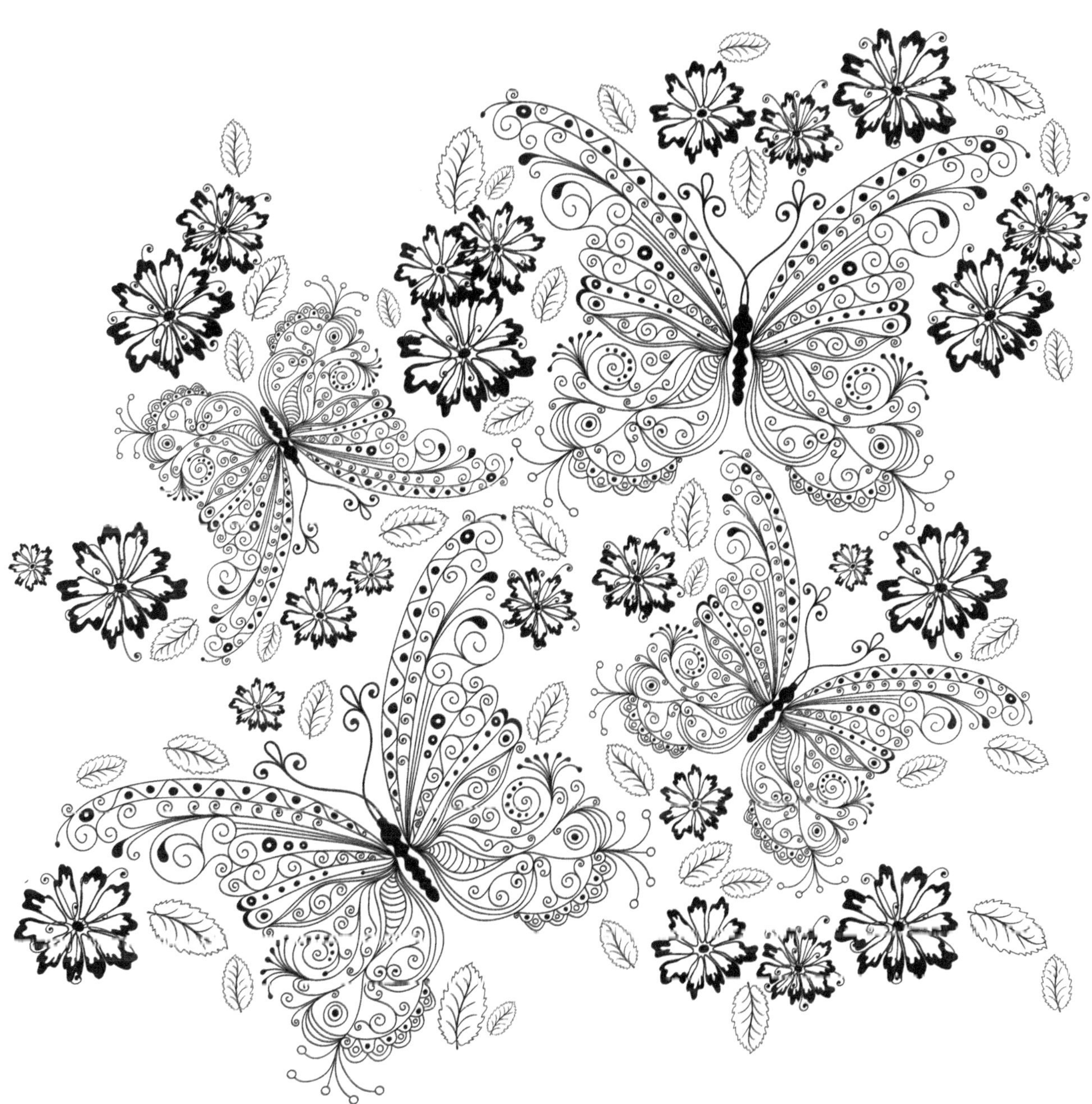

Creativity is allowing yourself to make mistakes.
Art is knowing which ones to keep.

- Scott Adams

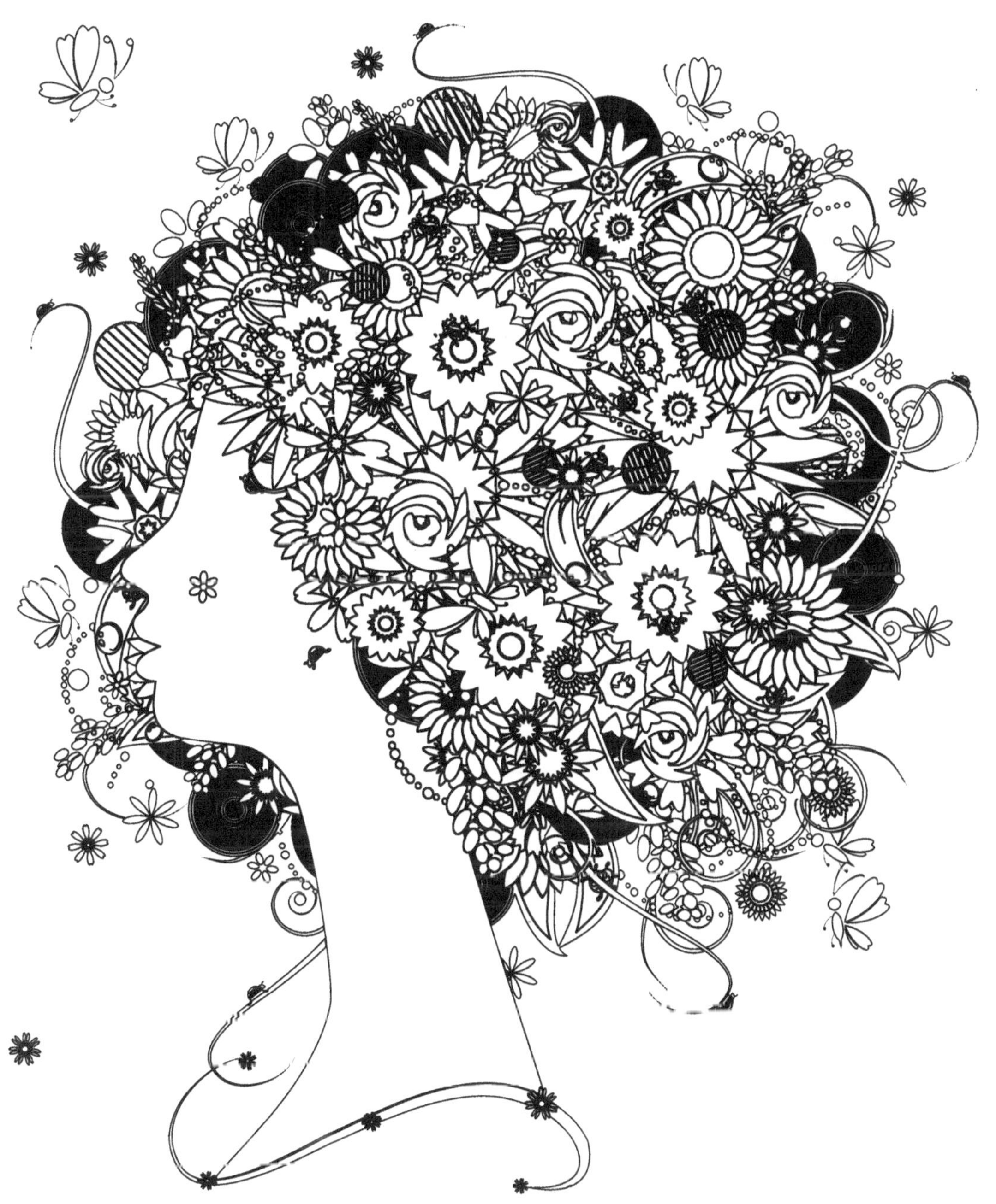

*Happiness is when
what you think,
what you say, and
what you do
are in harmony.*

– Mahatma Gandhi

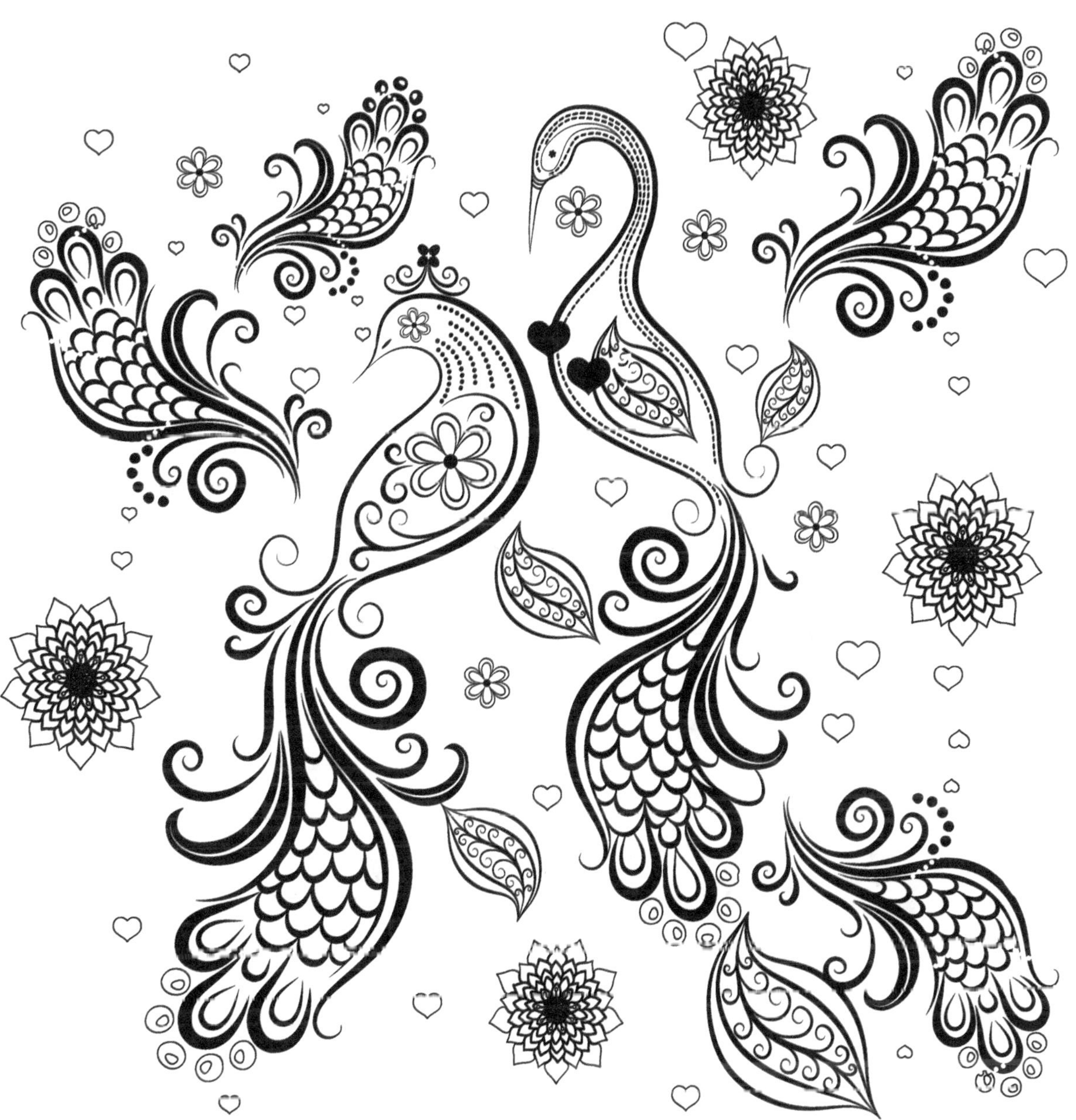

Let the wave of memory,
the storm of desire,
the fire of emotion
pass through
without affecting your equanimity.

– Sri Sathya Sai Baba

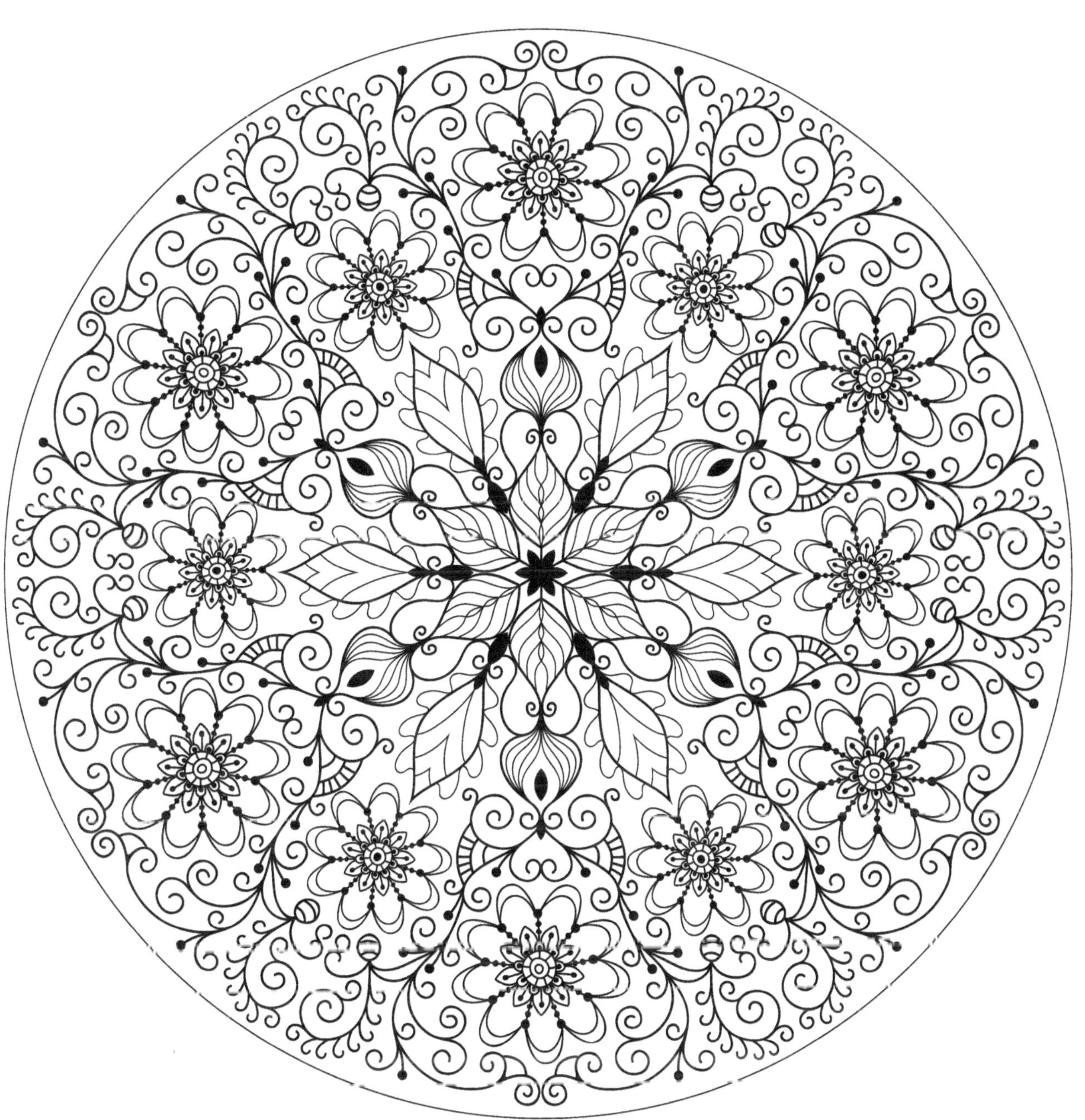

Acceptance doesn't mean resignation;
it means understanding that something is what it is
and that there's got to be a way through it.

— Michael J. Fox

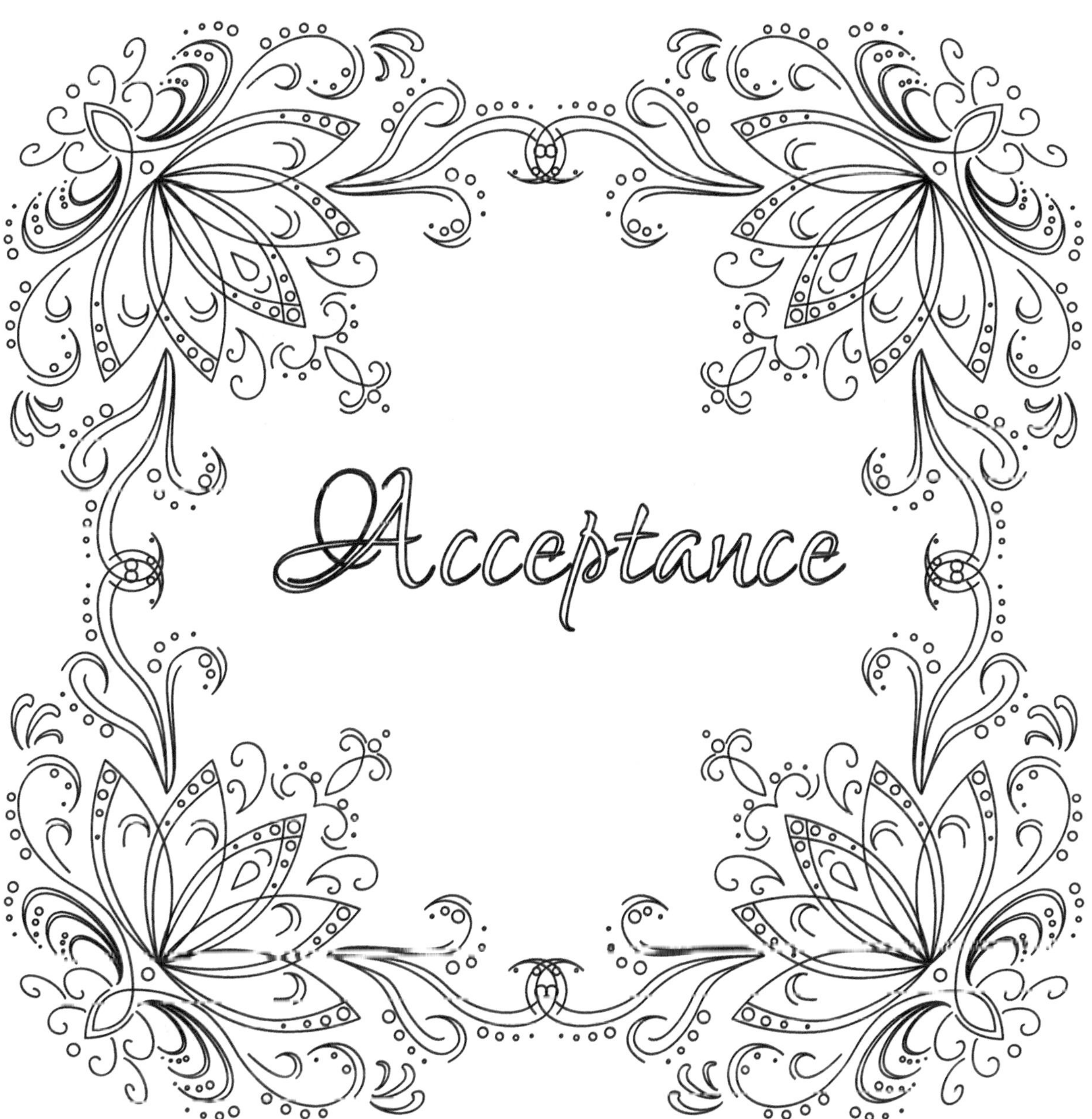

Acceptance

Perfectionism is not the same thing as striving to be your best. Perfectionism is the belief that if we live perfect, look perfect, and act perfect, we can minimize or avoid the pain of blame, judgement, and shame. It's a shield. It's a twenty-ton shield that we lug around thinking it will protect us when, in fact, it's the thing that's really preventing us from flight.

— Brené Brown, *The Gifts of Imperfection*

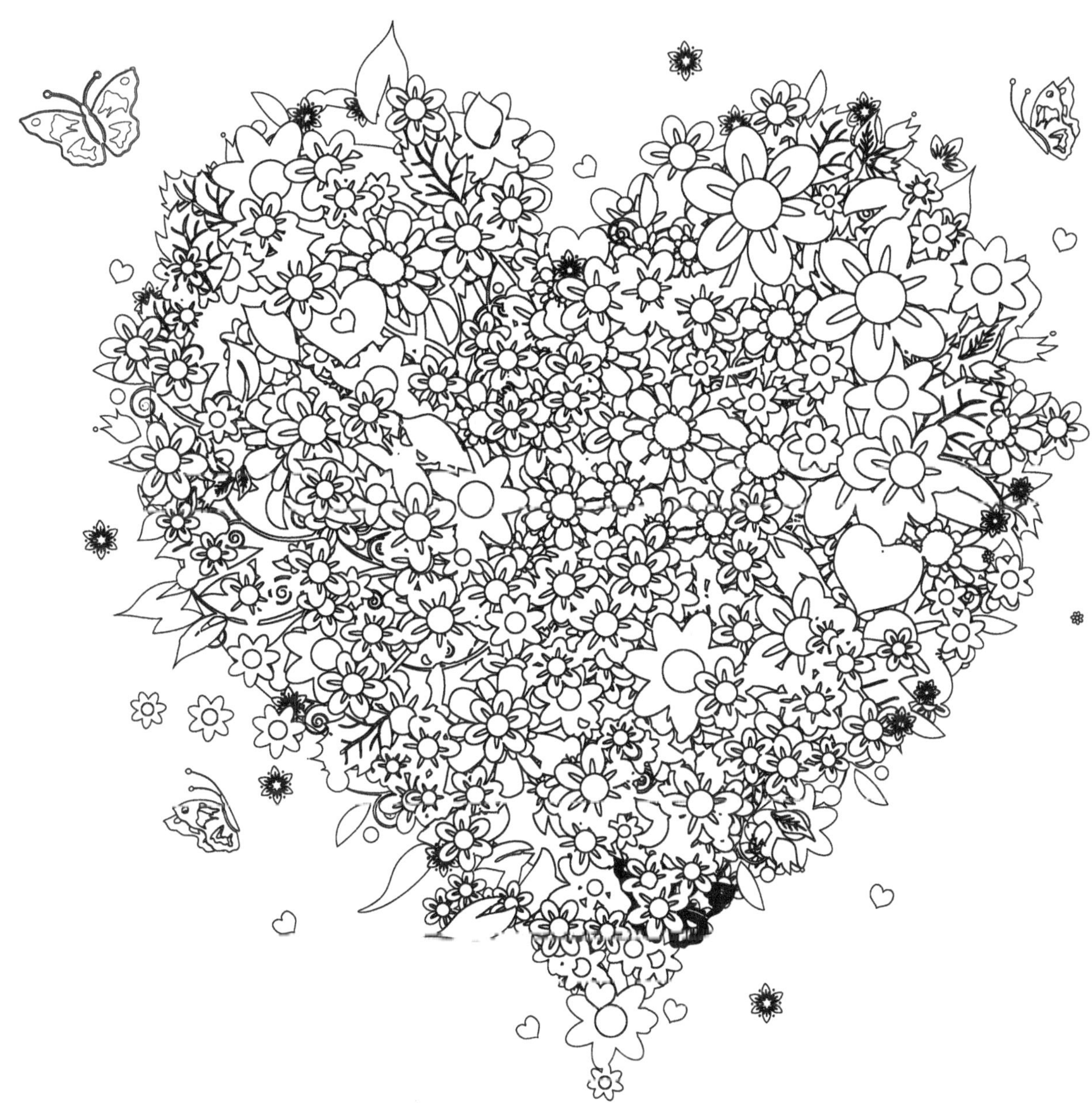

Show up in every single moment
like you're meant to be there.

\- Marie Forleo

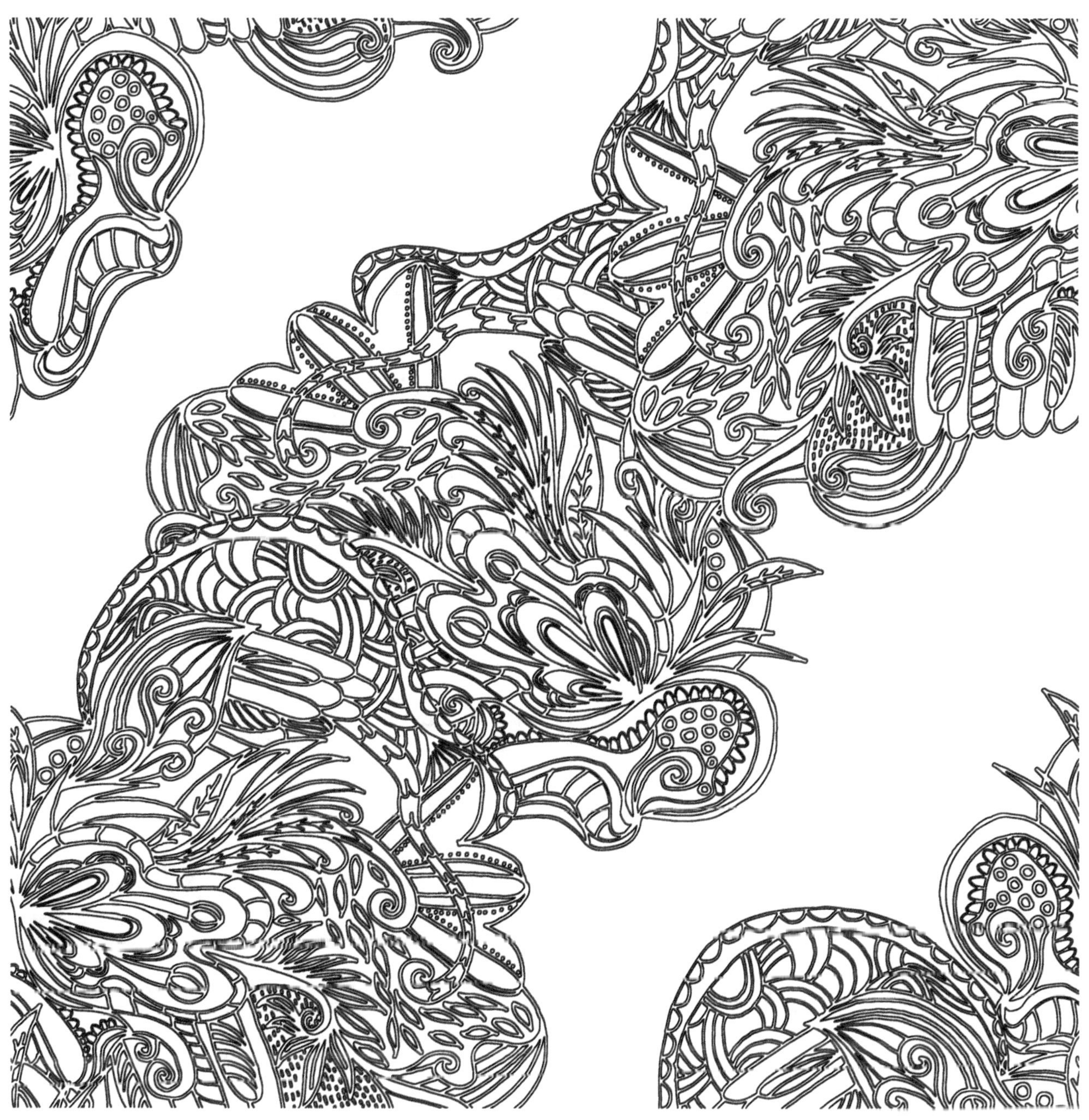

Simplicity boils down to two steps:
Identify the essential.
Eliminate the rest.

~ Leo Babauta

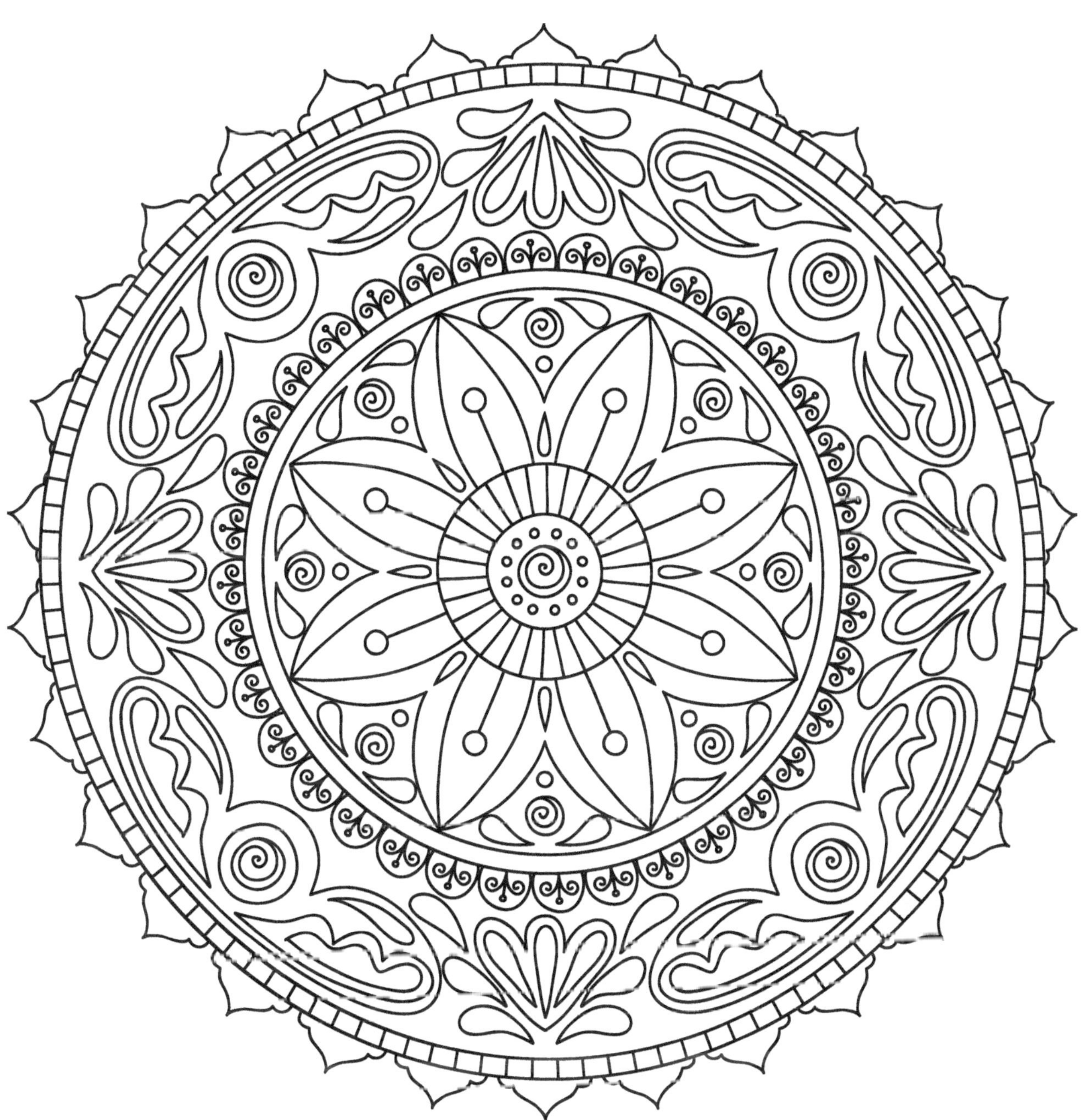

Be open to new experiences.
Just say yes.

— J.D. Roth

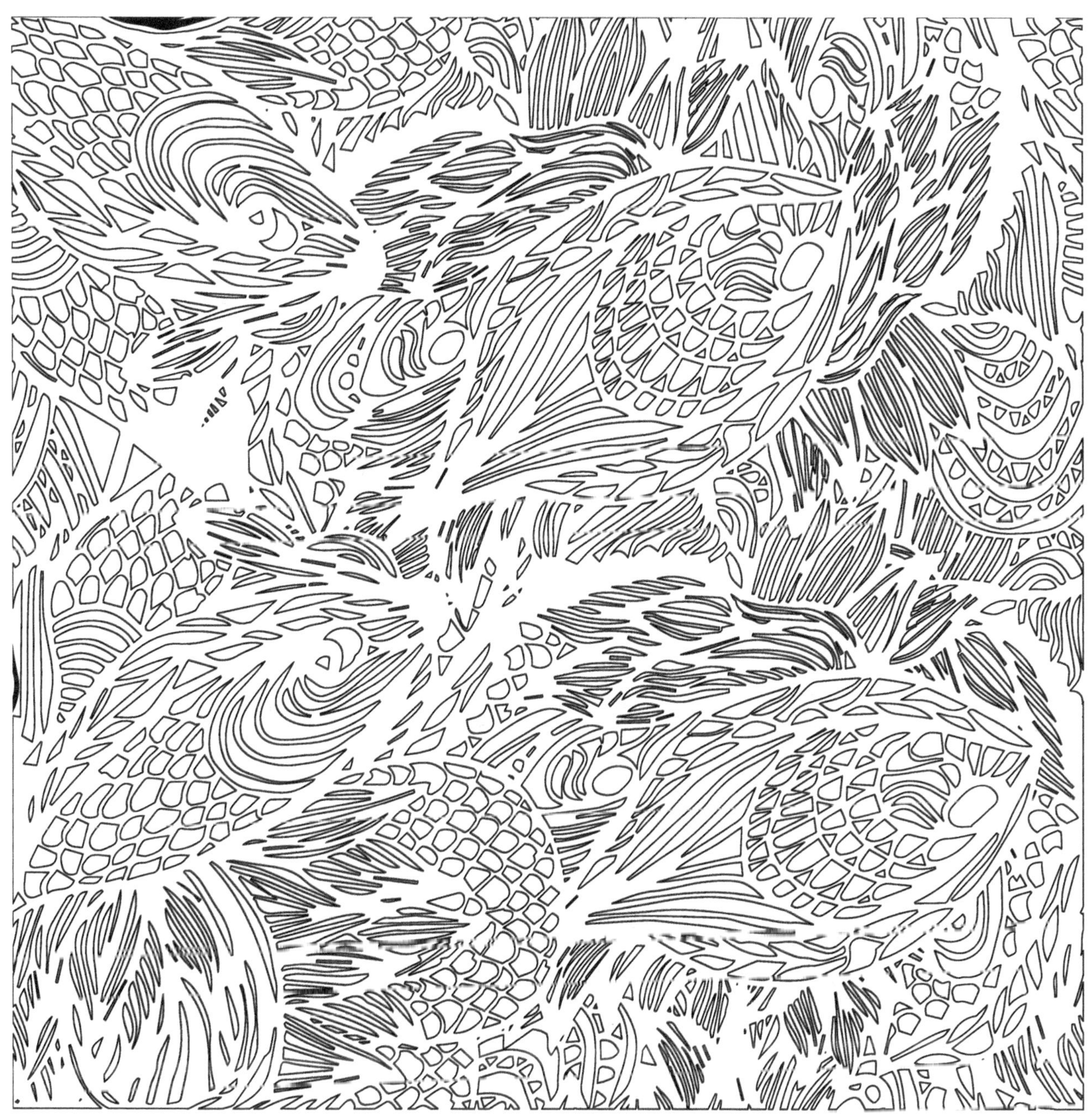

Nothing is harder to feel than joy because
we're so afraid it won't last.
We try to keep from getting caught off guard
because we think that will make it hurt less
when bad things happen.
Instead of dress-rehearsing disaster, practice gratitude.

– Brené Brown

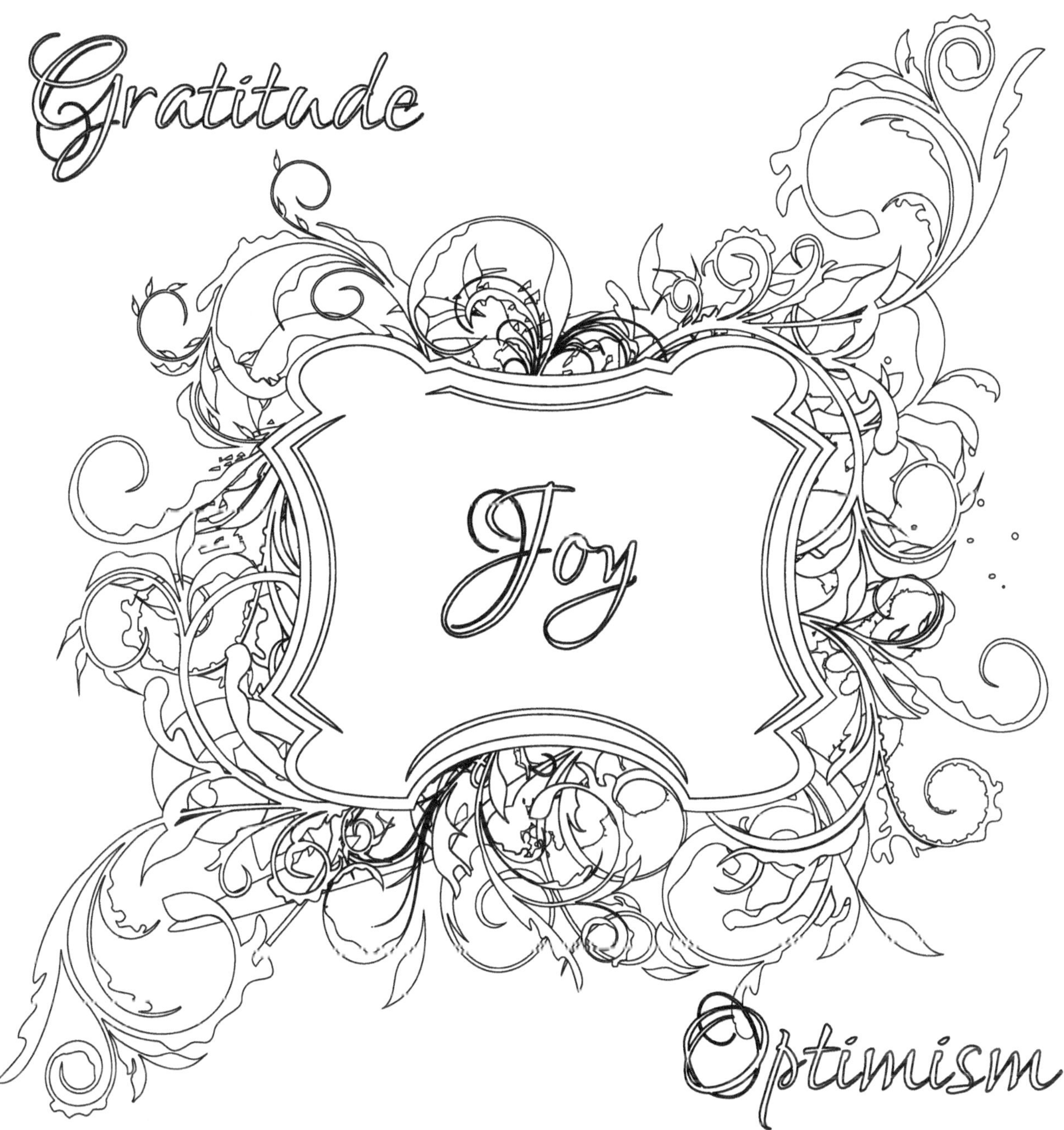

Gratitude
Joy
Optimism

I think that the ideal space must contain
elements of magic, serenity, sorcery and mystery.

– Luis Barragan

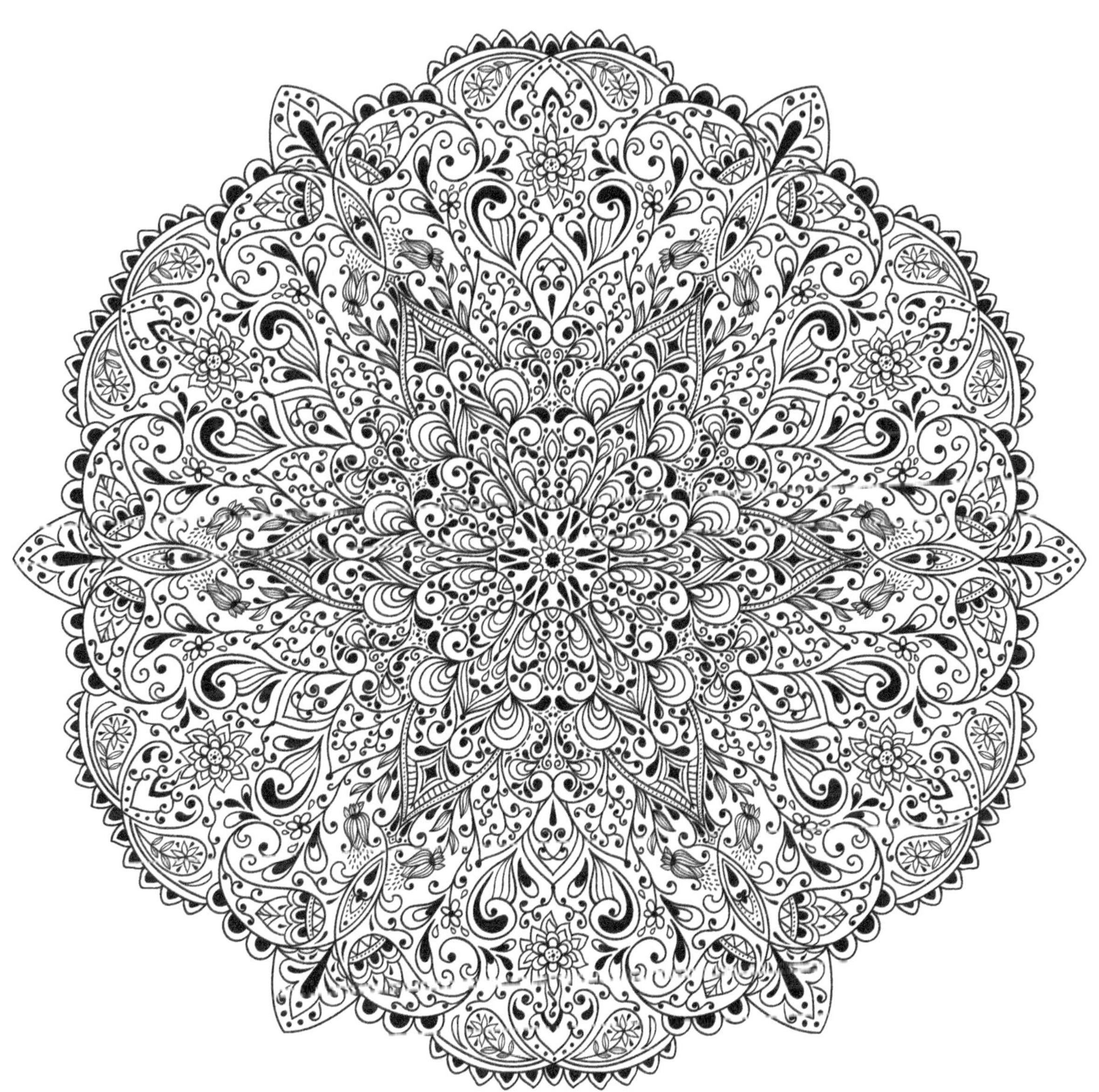

What do you do just for you?

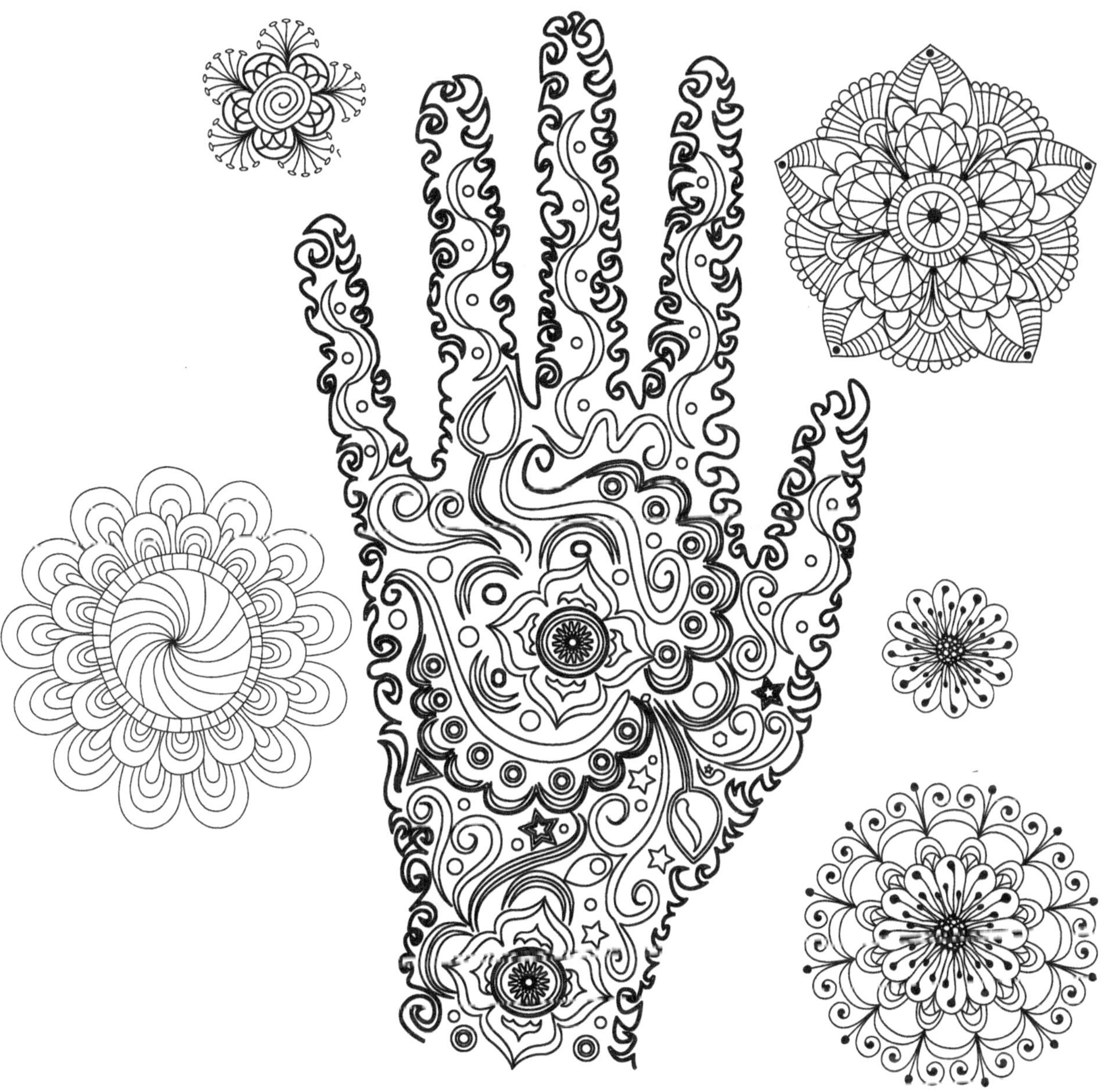

You are absolutely enough the way you are.

– Laurieann Gibson

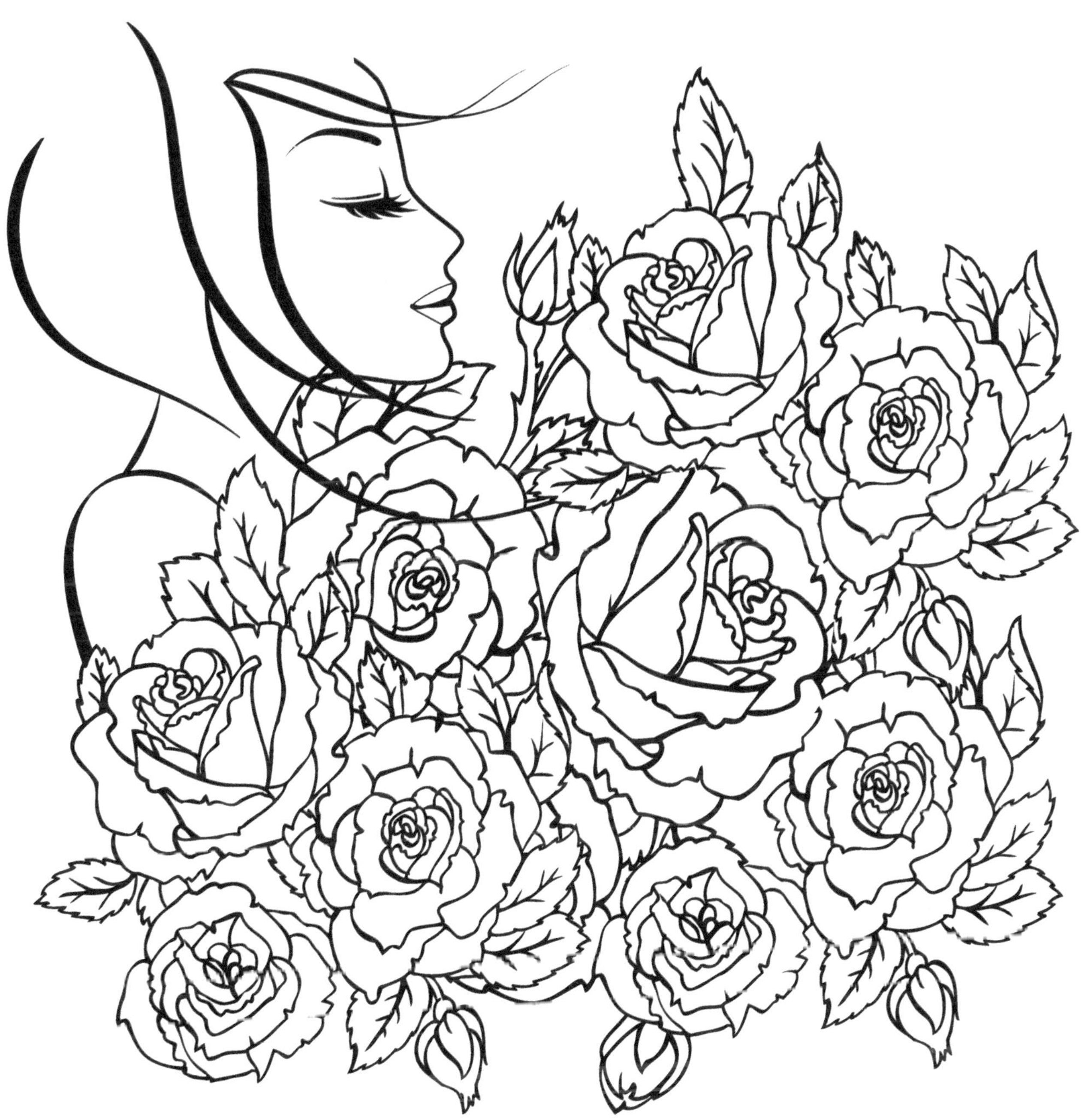

What are you grateful for?
(Try listing five things before you go to sleep each night)

I hope you've enjoyed this book! If you have, will you please leave a review on Amazon? It would really help me out.

If you'd like to read more about happiness and inspiration, I invite you to check out my blog. I have a free gift especially for readers of this book, available at:
http://17000-days.com/coloring

I hope you'll check it out and let me know what you think!

Many thanks!
Cara

Also by this author

How to be Happy (No Fairy Dust or Moonbeams Required)
Getting Unstuck
Reclaim Your Love: How to Fix Your Relationship